The Rt Revd Morris Maddocks was Founder-Director, with his wife Anne, of the Acorn Christian Healing Trust, and served as Adviser for the Ministry of Health and Healing to the Archbishops of Canterbury and York. His classic book, *The Christian Healing Ministry*, was first published by SPCK in 1981 and has remained in print ever since. Morris Maddocks died in January 2008.

God's Call to Heal

A life in music and healing

MORRIS MADDOCKS

First published in 2008

Society for Promoting Christian Knowledge
36 Causton Street
London SW1P 4ST

SPCK does not necessarily endorse the individual views contained in
its publications.

British Library Cataloguing-in-Publication Data
A catalogue record for this book is available from the British Library.

ISBN 978–0–281–05990–4

1 3 5 7 9 10 8 6 4 2

Designed and typeset by Kenneth Burnley, Wirral, Cheshire.
Printed in Great Britain by Ashford Colour Press

Produced on paper from sustainable forests

Contents

The plate section will be found between pages 96 and 97.

Publisher's note

At the time of his death, Morris Maddocks left a virtually complete manuscript. We have been as faithful as possible to this in producing *God's Call to Heal*.

Preface

The following is taken from a tribute to Bishop Morris Maddocks, given by Nicholas Frayling, the Dean of Chichester, at a Requiem Eucharist in Chichester Cathedral on 1 February 2008.

At the beginning of this Requiem Eucharist, Bishop John told us of his first reaction to the news of Morris's death, and the brief statement he asked to be read in the cathedral on the Sunday morning:

> Bishop Morris was like the Apostle Barnabas – always the encourager. I thank God for his long, distinctive and varied ministry.

There, you might think, is the sermon for today; but you would feel short-changed if I were to leave it at that. The truth is, ever since Morris's family asked me to preach at the Requiem, I have heard again Morris's voice in my ear, a few days before Anne's funeral:

'Tell them about her wonderful life, my dear, and don't forget to mention God!'

To which I would want to add . . . 'and Christian healing'.

As is well known in these parts, Morris married Anne Sheail in 1955, here in the cathedral – at 8.30 in the morning, incidentally, so that the choristers would not miss their lessons, no doubt much to their disappointment. Anne had become Assistant Organist to Horace Hawkins in 1942. Their marriage lasted 51 years, and was a true partnership of the heart, and also the gospel.

Morris was ordained in London Diocese and served his title at St Peter's, Ealing, under Henry Cooper: 'Not the boxer,' he would say, but a distinguished Prebendary who was himself a pioneer of the Christian healing movement. This was followed by a second curacy at St Andrew's, Uxbridge, and it is recorded that Morris's individual sense of humour began to make itself known. There were two ladies called Mrs Green in that parish, each with different coloured hair. Morris called them 'Mrs Light Green and Mrs Dark Green'. He would say, if you forgot something, 'Well, I told you, but perhaps you were not in the room at the time.'

Increasingly, Morris and Anne were drawn towards the ministry of healing. He never claimed to have any personal gifts as a healer, but he became increasingly convinced of the benefit of building close links between the Church and the medical profession, placing healing at the heart of the Church's mission. He first publicly expounded these ideas in his most influential book, *The Christian Healing Ministry*, which was published in 1981. He said, 'I felt my hand was guided when I wrote that book.'

After 11 years [as Bishop of Selby], Morris and Anne became convinced that God was calling them to a new kind of ministry that would enable them to concentrate on the ministry of healing. Archbishop Stuart Blanch created a new post for Morris as 'Special Adviser to the Archbishops of Canterbury and York on Health and Healing'. There was no salary, but it was Anne who uttered the now famous words, 'God will provide' – and so, somehow, he did.

Morris set about establishing a network of healing advisers in every diocese in England. As is well known, his work led to the formation of the Acorn Christian Healing Foundation, which has grown, as the name implies, from a very modest beginning to a worldwide institution, encompassing a ministry of listening, the healing of people and communities, and the reconciliation of individuals and peoples. Acorn now has partnerships in ten nations. Morris was very proud of its achievements, as he was of his association with Burrswood, of whose founder, Dorothy Kerin, he was the biographer.

Morris was honoured for his work for healing in the Church by the award of the Templeton Prize and the Medal of St Augustine.

He retired in 1995, and kept a promise to bring Anne back to Chichester. During her last year or two of life, when he spent all his energy caring for her, Morris prayed for strength – indeed, that the cup of suffering might be lifted from them.

He drew strength most of all from the sacrament of the Holy Eucharist, secure in the knowledge that, whenever we take the bread and wine, we are linked to the sacrifice of Jesus. More than that, we are joined with the great company of God's people who have been redeemed and healed, and we ourselves are strengthened to live and promote his healing in all the circumstances of our daily lives.

The hymn we shall sing during Communion expressed for Morris the outworking of this profound conviction:

> Take my will, and make it Thine;
> it shall be no longer mine.

If it had occurred to me, we might also have sung Thomas Chisholme's words, unfashionable these days perhaps, but which come near to expressing the heart of Morris's faith, and the mission to which he dedicated the greater part of his life:

Living for Jesus who died in my place,
Bearing on Calvary my sin and disgrace;
Such love constrains me to answer his call,
Follow his leading and give him my all.

May he rest in peace, and be raised in glory. Amen.

Chapter 1

Beginnings

Anne

Anne was born Nellie Anne Sheail on 23 October 1911, four months after the Coronation of King George V and Queen Mary. The magnificent ceremony in Westminster Abbey, which included a march specially composed by Edward Elgar, took place during a period of great industrial and politcal unrest: 70,000 transport workers were on strike in Liverpool, while the votes-for-women suffragette movement would shortly commit its first act of arson. Even more worrying was the increasing turbulence abroad, especially in western Europe. So divided was the region that the assassination of Franz Ferdinand in Sarajevo three years later would be sufficient to spark off the disastrous events leading to the First World War.

This all seemed a little remote from the peace and permanence of the Sussex Downs, where Anne's family had lived in Heyshott for many generations. They had been well-to-do farmers, but lost most of their money when a daughter of the house took to banking the farm income in her own account instead of her father's, then went off and got married! Anne's father was part of a large family, and there is still a house in Heyshott owned by descendants of his younger sister, Nan Dudley. He and Nan were very close to each other, as we are still to her family there. Anne's paternal grandfather was a gamekeeper on Lord Leconfield's (Petworth) estate nearby, and her parents were married in the chapel of Wiston House, a magnificent sixteenth-century manor which is itself now licensed for weddings. Both of Anne's parents were violinists, and their music-making would prove to be an enormous influence on her.

When Anne was five her father took the post of manager at the Bignor Park farm, further east along the Downs. Gradually the family became immersed in the life of the parish of Sutton with Bignor under a fine vicar called Newman, who was influenced by the Tractarian movement and taught Anne the catholic faith as held by the Church of England. Anne went to the local school but learned the piano and violin at home, and was only a young teenager when she was appointed organist of both Sutton and Bignor churches. She earned the princely sum of ten pounds per annum! The experience sowed the seeds of a great love for the organ which never left her: 'The violin was never me,' she said later, 'I wanted something bigger.' She did in fact try the double bass, the advantage being (she thought) that she could hide behind it if she played a wrong note!

Anne's father provided musical accompaniment for the village folk-dance team, and Anne and her fellow dancers were taught by Mr Rolt, a physical education teacher in Brighton, whose strict discipline, softened only by the sheer kindness of his wife, was to reap dividends. (Years later we were delighted to discover Mrs Rolt living as the tenant of Elgar's Cottage, Brinkwells, near Fittleworth.) The team took part in local competitions and, with Anne and her dancing partner as leaders, they soon became county champions, thus qualifying for the national championships. The young dancers' first trip to London was a great excitement, and

Anne remembers how small she felt in the vast arena of the Albert Hall. The team won the national championship at the second attempt, and, to end the afternoon, Anne and her partner were asked to do a special dance with the Northumberland pair who had been runners-up. As a result, they were invited to give demonstrations in the grounds of many big houses and rectories. Anne would often travel with Tony Bertram and his fiancée Barbara Randolph on these expeditions, sitting in the dickey of their small sports car. Barbara (who had been her Guide captain) and Tony eventually married and lived in the farm adjacent to Bignor church. Tony was in MI5, and during the war the farmhouse was used as a transit camp for French Resistance fighters. The villagers thought Mrs Bertram was having a lot of lodgers!

Anne's parents worked very hard in Lord Mersey's employ. The house was entrusted to them during the family's frequent long absences, and Anne's mother had to clean it right through whenever the family was due to return. Anne inherited her efficiency and aptitude for hard work, but as the years went on she felt that her whole being was filled with music and had to find a way of expressing it. Though she loved her home, she knew she had to move on and have training in order to express her talents. She also longed to be married, but deep in the country her choice was limited.

Unfortunately she made a hasty marriage as a way out. It was not a happy one, and eventually her husband died of wounds received in the Second World War. His service in the forces did give her the freedom to pursue her great love of music, and one day in 1938 she took a bus to Chichester and called (unannounced) on the cathedral organist, H. A. Hawkins. He was a pupil of the famous French organist, composer and teacher, Charles-Marie Widor (1844–1957) – Anne had learned always to go to the top! – and 'Hawkey', as he was known, agreed to take her on as an articled pupil, together with Geoffrey Barnard. She and Geoffrey would remain friends ever afterwards.

Being an articled pupil involved a hard routine for two years. Once a week Anne would be up very early, cycle to her parents' home two miles away with her pet Pekingese in the pannier, leave the dog, cycle home, jump off her bike, and walk another mile for the bus to Chichester. There she would have her lesson on the cathedral organ, practise until mid-afternoon (with a break for a pork pie for lunch) and then return home. She had pedals fitted to her piano so that she could do several hours a day 'organ' practice, involving pedal technique.

When the war started, Hawkey's German maids were interned, so he asked Anne if she would come and live in a flat he had made at 2 St Richard's Walk and add housekeeping duties to her music. (He promised to teach her French cooking!) Anne readily agreed because she wanted to watch Hawkey at the organ, especially on Sunday mornings when his improvisations were an inspiration. He began to teach her the Clara Schumann method to perfect her technique, and she practised hard, often into the night. Hawkey soon realized that Anne had the ability and aptitude to play and interpret Widor's music as the master would have wanted. In fact she revelled in all the French music for which Chichester was becoming famous. She felt happy and fulfilled.

Less than two years later, on Easter Day 1942, Hawkey appointed Anne his assistant, presenting her with a copy of Vierne's First Symphony. The periodical *Choir and Organ* recently had a note about female organists and declared that Anne had been the first female assistant organist in an English cathedral.

Only a year after she had become assistant organist, Hawkey felt that Anne was ready to play a big work and managed somehow, in the middle of a war in which France was occupied by Germany, to get hold of the music for the Poulenc Organ Concerto. He gave Anne the organ score to master, while he trained his small cathedral orchestra. Their faithful and exciting performance of the work in May 1943 was the first in the UK, and received a mention in the *Musical Times*. At a repeat performance of the concerto the following year, Boris Ord, organist and choirmaster of King's College, Cambridge, asked if he could listen in the organ loft. Anne told him firmly, 'Yes, but only if you sit on that chair and don't move!'

In 1945, just after VE Day, there was another musical occasion. The *Musical Times* records:

> Widor's Mass for two choirs with organ, strings, trumpets and trombones was sung at a special service on June 24th in Chichester cathedral. The cathedral choir was augmented by members of the Arundel Choral Society and girls from St Michael's school and trombone players were drawn from the band of HMS *Collingwood* and the strings were those of the cathedral orchestra. Anne Sheail was at the organ. The cathedral choir also sang Widor's *Ave Verum* which was written for and dedicated to Mr H. A. Hawkins the cathedral organist who conducted.

Other cathedral organists began to come down, now that Chichester was on the musical map. There was great interest in French music, which was not well known and rarely performed at the time. Chichester also became famous for its Tudor music and for the singing of the psalms to plainsong three times a week. Hawkey had been an articled pupil of Solesmes and made regular trips to Quarr Abbey on the Isle of Wight to check his training and performance of the chant with their musician, Dom Desroquettes. Of the organists of the time, Boris Ord of King's College, Cambridge, was already at hand, serving in the RAF at Tangmere. He became a frequent visitor, getting into a routine of Evensong, a drink in the Dolphin, supper at 2 St Richard's Walk, and a session on the organ with Anne. He was so absorbed in the music that he often missed the last bus back to camp and had to walk. With Tangmere only a couple of miles from the city, there were frequent dog-fights overhead in the early years of the war, and the Close residents were meant to go into an air raid shelter in the bishop's garden when the sirens sounded. However, they always chose the stairs up to the cathedral chapter house. On fire-watching nights, one of Anne's tasks was to help carry Hawkey's mattress to the fire-watching room so that he could rest when off duty.

Another organist, Sir William Harris of Windsor, appeared fairly regularly. On his first visit, early on in Hawkey's time at Chichester, a verger had engaged him in conversation. 'This new organist', he said, 'can't half make the instrument sing, but the last one was neither fit to play the organ than you nor me sir!' Sir William used to love to tell the story against himself. When he heard of Anne's performance of the Poulenc concerto, he invited her to his house in Windsor and sat her down at the Steinway piano in his drawing room with the organ score, while he took the full orchestral score to the other Steinway. Anne knew every note of the concerto and was amazed at how brilliantly he sight-read it. Afterwards they played to each other on the organ in St George's Chapel.

Other organists followed, including William McKie of Westminster Abbey, George Thalben-Ball of the Temple and Harold Darke of St Michael's Cornhill. One of the most regular visitors to St Richard's Walk was Sir Arnold Bax, at the time the Master of the King's Music. He lived at the White Horse Inn in Storrington, where there is now a plaque on the wall to mark his residence. He loved the ride along the Downs to Amberley and would always sit at the top of the bus to gain a better view. He dedicated a Nunc Dimittis to Hawkey, and it was first performed in 1947, the *Musical Times* of September that year recording the following:

> At a special service of Music on July 20, the augmented choir of Chichester cathedral combined with the Bognor Choral Society and the Bognor Training College in a performance of Bax's *Te Deum* and *Nunc Dimittis* at which the composer was present. The programme included motets by Allegri and Blow and the Allegro from Widor's Symphony No. 6 for organ and three trombones. Anne Sheail was at the organ and H. A. Hawkins conducted.

About this time, Hawkey sent Anne on a tour of the Paris organ lofts with Geoffrey Barnard, now home from the war. They were equipped with personal letters from Hawkey to the Paris organists, whom he knew well, and with letters of introduction to certain friends. One was M. de Vallombrosa in the Rue de Grenelle, two doors away from the headquarters of the Gestapo, who little knew that their choirmaster neighbour was the treasurer of the Resistance and kept its funds under the pedal board of the church organ. Anne was very pleased to make the acquaintance of two famous French female organists, Jean Demessier of Sacré Coeur, and Rolande Fancinelli. On her tour of cathedrals in the north of England the previous year, 1946, she met among others Goss-Custard of Liverpool, Malcolm Boyle of Chester and Dr Moody of Ripon. She also called on Sir Edward Bairstow in York but he was too ill to see her. Sadly he died later that year. Anne realized that these visits were an integral part of her musical education and was inspired by watching so many great musicians at work.

After the war, on the initiative of Bishop Bell, the theological college returned to Chichester. The students included many of the war veterans who had received a vocation during their time in the forces, and others who had done their National Service. Hawkey involved the college choir especially in French music such as the Widor *Mass* and Tantum Ergo which were written for two choirs, four parts and men's (seminarium) voices. Festivals, including the college festival, and Refreshment Sunday, were great occasions for this double choir music, and from this point on Hawkey imported trumpet and trombone players from the band of the Royal Marines. They appreciated Anne's performance at the organ, as she appreciated their skill in playing, mostly without rehearsing together.

There was to be a third performance of the Poulenc concerto, together with Widor's *Salvum Fac Populum Tuum*, while Hawkey played the finale of Widor's Symphony No. 6 in an arrangement by himself for organ and trombones. There were also organ solos. This time Hawkey was brave enough to invite the London critics down. Archibald Farmer, the most famous of them all, came up to the organ loft after the concert and told Anne he had greatly enjoyed it, but his position in the cathedral was not the best place in which to have heard the Poulenc piece, and could she please perform it again. She replied, 'Yes, but you must ask the conductor and orchestra if they are willing to play it again.' Off he went and asked them, and they agreed. Afterwards there were again footsteps on the organ stairs. Archibald Farmer came up, this time with Felix Aprahamian on one of his first assignments as a music critic, and presented Anne with his full score of the work, congratulated her and took her out to tea! With her usual humour she later said, 'Pity it wasn't dinner.' Archibald Farmer's piece appeared in the *Musical Times*:

> The organ was shared between Mr Hawkins and his assistant Anne Sheail, the latter playing when the former conducted, with quite indistinguishable excellence. Anne Sheail's part in the exacting Poulenc score was beautifully rhythmical, in spite of the fact that it was impossible for her to see the conductor, and her handling of the difficult and antiquated instrument won much praise . . . The organ at Chichester, although not old enough to be historic, is a voice from the past and the surprising thing is that it sounded equally at home in Tudor and modern French styles . . . For good measure Mr Hawkins repeated the Poulenc at the end of the afternoon and we left Chichester greatly in debt to him and Anne Sheail.

In 1953 I came down from Cambridge to the theological college and immediately realized I was in for a feast of music. I was not familiar with much French music, and what I heard in the cathedral opened my eyes and ears to a new and glorious sound. I came to know and appreciate Hawkey's and Anne's musicianship and received encouragement and help from them both, especially after I was appointed the college organist. The musical atmosphere created to enhance the worship in the cathedral was an inspiration to us all; in particular, Hawkey's improvising after the Gospel and at the Offertory at the High Mass.

Anne and I began what was to become a very deep friendship. Music was the initial attraction, and we have always looked back on our time in the organ loft together as the beginning of our relationship. When time allowed, we played tennis together and later on I taught her squash, both of which she enjoyed. When my father died, a very great blow to me just before my ordination, Anne, on her own initiative, came all the way up to Yorkshire for the funeral. She had met my father on one of her northern tours and also on visits to Chichester. She and Hawkey very generously had my mother and me for Christmas that year. Anne was interested to find that my mother was a pianist, and we all got on well. Just as I was keen to learn from Anne's musicianship and teaching – and she appreciated that I was musical and able to learn some of the French music – so Anne was keen to deepen her spirituality and life of prayer. She asked me to buy an office book for her, and whenever possible we said the Church's daily offices together, a practice we continued regularly until the end of her life.

Anne was immersed in the very full musical life of the cathedral and through her skill in performance (she frequently had to read scores written for two organs, and Hawkey's compositions with the ink still wet) and her total sensitivity towards, and resonance with, Hawkey, she contributed to a sound which many travelled from far and wide to hear. Even Swedish TV came to film the choir in performance and the organists at leisure in the garden of 2 St Richard's Walk. BBC TV was to broadcast live the High Mass on Easter Day in 1955, Anne's final Easter Day and thirteenth anniversary of her appointment as assistant cathedral organist. She and I knew that God was working in us both, and we were to marry later in the year, music having played a major part in forming our relationship and creating the deep love we shared.

Morris

The best description of Elland was uttered in Canterbury railway station by no less a person than the then Archdeacon of Canterbury, Bernard Pawley, as he and I chatted together while waiting for the London train. We were joined by one of the most learned clergymen in the Church of England, David Edwards, who enquired how we knew each other. When I explained that Bernard had followed my father as Rector of Elland, David asked, 'Where on earth is that?' Out of the side of his mouth Bernard muttered, 'Shall we educate this ignorant fellow?', then said to David in his broadest Yorkshire, 'For your information, Elland is the place what keeps 'alifax and 'uddersfield apart.' It caused a few stares from fellow travellers.

Elland is in fact situated in the old West Riding of Yorkshire by the River Calder. An industrial woollen town and home of the Gannex raincoat (worn most notably by the Huddersfield-born Prime Minister, Harold Wilson), it also produced durable flagstones which were transported all over the country via the canal that runs alongside the river. Elland's other claim to fame (rather more appreciated by me as a boy) was its traditional sweet factory, Dobsons, which is still thriving today. Mr Dobson used to fashion a pipe for me from the sweet mixture and I would 'smoke' it at home to be like my father. Everything in the town was black – churches, houses, schools, and especially the mill buildings and chimneys of which I could count 47 from one point in our garden. I was often that colour myself and had to be scrubbed before meals. But with its industrial smog, smell of shoddy, noisy mills and genial, smiling people, Elland was home. I had a happy childhood there.

I was born in the rectory on 28 April 1928. As was usual on a Saturday afternoon, my father was on the golf course and had to be hailed to take the doctor's phone call. 'I have delivered the bishop, and your wife is doing well', was the somewhat prophetic message.

It was probably not surprising that my father served most of his ministry in Yorkshire, having grown up mainly in nearby Manchester, where my grandfather, who was a Shakespearian scholar, ran a bookshop. After attending Manchester Grammar School, my father and the next brother down, Leslie – who was also godfather to me and later Archdeacon of Zanzibar – went to Oxford, where my father fell under the successors of the Oxford Movement. He was to remain on the catholic side of the Church throughout his ministry. All my mother's family, on the other hand, were of the Evangelical tradition. My grandfather, Edmund Sharpe, was Rector at Bishop's Waltham in Hampshire, and it was there that my mother met my father when he came to preach on behalf of the National Society. In contrast to my grandfather's missionary childhood, my grandmother, Theresa Peareth-Kincaid-Lennox, was brought up in Lennox Castle near Glasgow, and my mother could recall playing in its endless corridors before the First World War. Today its grounds house Celtic Football Club's new training complex.

My father was 48 when he and my mother were married at Bishop's Waltham in 1926. His first wife had died in childbirth many years previously, and the memorial plaque that he placed in the sanctuary of her parish church, St Edith's, Bishop Wilton, near York, is just above the bishop's chair. In later years I would sit below it when Anne and I visited the parish.

It must have been quite a culture shock for my mother to be brought from the clean and serene pastures of Hampshire to the industrial smog of the West Riding. On many days we had to take a twopenny tram ride up Ainleys Hill just to see the sun! But love is a wonderful thing and my mother was an essentially cheerful person who made a happy home for my father and me. In the early days I used to go everywhere with her, on all her visits to friends and parishioners and even on her speaking engagements to Mothers' Union branches. Annesley House, where Aunty Eleanor and (adopted) Aunty Christine Walker lived, had a very large fender around the fire, and it was my delight to unscrew all the brass knobs and dismantle it. Mercifully my Meccano skills enabled me to put it together again. But Heptonstall, where Sylvia Plath is buried, was my favourite place: it had a nice large horse-trough where I could sail my boat.

My mother played the piano well, and from the earliest days I was influenced by music, which was to be my initial connecting link with Anne. My father's influence was also profound. Perhaps because of the sadness of his earlier life, he became a most sensitive and caring priest, something which I admired and wanted to emulate. Apparently my first very audible utterance in church was, 'I want to be a cergyman (*sic*) and peach (*sic*) like Daddy'. I both loved and stood in awe of him. He never had to be cross with me: one look was sufficient. He always said I inherited his sensitivity, and we were close to one another.

During my childhood I was also very fond of 'Olly' who, as a mill girl of 15, had called at the house and said she had been told by her supervisor that she wouldn't get to heaven if she wasn't baptized, 'So could I be baptized, now if possible, because I want to go to heaven.' She came from a pagan home with a drunken brother and her mother smoked a pipe. My father told her she would have to come to classes for six months. 'What on earth for?' she asked, but eventually agreed. She became a pillar of the Church, and when her mother died, entered a convent, one of many vocations fostered by my father among the young of the parish. Twice a week she would come to play with me, and later on accompanied me to my father's catechism class on Sundays.

My father's curates were all great fun and enjoyed life, like my parents. One was Felix Arnott who later became Archbishop of Brisbane and retired to Chichester. On one Christmas Day my father was unwell and Felix took the main service at the parish church. He began his sermon, 'Behold I bring you good tidings of great joy! Oh, the rector is ill and sends his greetings'! The congregation dissolved. Another was Theodore Mathieson who later gave his life to minister in the Oxford Mission to Calcutta. He taught me to serve at the altar and was a person of great enthusiasm, always rubbing his hands and declaring, 'Marvellous – terrific – superb' – the word would change each week.

Until I was eight, I attended the local church day school, but the Elland smog began to affect my lungs, and it was decided I would be sent to a preparatory school in Surrey. I was miserable being so far away from my parents and the home I loved, but I eventually settled down and did fairly well at schoolwork and games, thanks to some good teachers. Among them was a Mr Lock, our French master, who was shaped like a pear and inevitably called 'Le Poivre'. (He called me 'Le Boeuf' – the ox!) He had most of us speaking French by the time we left, and his scripture lessons made the Old Testament come alive: I could always remember every detail of the stories. A year after the war began, the school was hit by a landmine, which blew the couple who occupied the lodge – still in their bed – into the garden. They were shocked but mercifully unscathed. After that, we were all evacuated to Devonshire.

Childhood holidays were mostly spent in the south with my mother's relations. My Aunt Rosie had married a prison governor, a great character with a wooden leg who, when he was courting my aunt in Scotland, was asked by her grandmother at Lennox, 'How do you find the air up here, Commander Tabuteau?' He replied, 'Very embracing, ma'am.' I had my fourth birthday in Pentonville prison, measles at 12 in Oxford prison, and enjoyed holidays in Southsea, when Uncle Reggie moved to the prison in Portsmouth. It was a useful experience to mention in my later prison ministry.

I was very fond of my dear cousin Nina – mother of Helen, who was to be such a support to me in later years – and thanks to Nina's financial help, was able to go on to the parsons' sons public school, St John's, Leatherhead. There I was influenced by the integrity and pastoral care of both the headmaster, J. S. Carter, and my housemaster, J. C. Hammond, a brilliant history teacher and rugby coach. Bishop Walter Carey, one of this world's saints, prepared me for confirmation. He had been a rugby international and I recall him pushing our second row off their feet in his cassock! I preferred the sports field to the classroom myself – I was in the first teams for rugby and cricket for two years – and with many of the staff away in the forces and older men coming in, I did not work as hard as I should have done.

However, one day the headmaster said to me, 'Somehow we have got to get you a scholarship to university.' By this time I really wanted to be ordained and we discovered that there was a scholarship for ordinands at Trinity College, Cambridge, which was awarded by the Bishop of London. I volunteered that my great-uncle was the Archdeacon of London. (I had often stayed with him at 9 Amen Court, where a favourite pastime was being hauled upstairs and down in the food lift operated by the maids.) The headmaster jumped at this information, and after an interview with Bishop William Wand, who later ordained me, I was awarded the scholarship. Before I could take it up, I was called for National Service.

The Duke of Wellington's was my first regiment, and in later years I was always glad to meet soldiers visiting the Regimental Chapel in York Minster. I went on to Catterick with the Royal Signals and experienced there the terrible winter of 1947, when the snow lay so long and so deep that people began to wonder if another ice age had begun! Here I attended a selection board for a commission and was asked what I thought they were looking for in a potential officer. 'A sense of humour, sir,' I replied, not sure if this would help my case, but I passed. (I was pleased to read recently that General Sir Mike Jackson, in his address at a Sandhurst Sovereign's parade, said that, after all the other qualities needed to be an officer, it was essential to maintain a sense of humour.) Next stop was the Officer Cadet Training Unit at Aldershot under the formidable Regimental Sergeant Major 'Tubby' Brittain to gain a king's commission, and a posting with the Royal Army Service Corps to Berlin at the time of the airlift. The Russians were being rather unpleasant during the early period of the Cold War and had closed all rail and road links, which meant the only way out of the British, French and American sectors was by air. One day all officers were summoned to the Olympic stadium that Hitler had built for the 1936 games. The General briefed us that the Russians had crashed one of their planes in our sector and had brought in troops to surround it. He then said, 'I have surrounded them with our troops and told them I shall fire if they don't get out within 24 hours.' It was a brave move and might have sparked the Third World War, but mercifully the Russians got out after 22 hours. Confrontation was the only language they understood.

In Berlin I made great friends with Martin Mackintosh, a subaltern in the nearby transport section, who was the youngest son of the Mackintosh Toffee dynasty. We had actually lived within three miles of one another all our lives without meeting. Martin didn't write many letters, so his parents were always ringing up mine to garner the news from Berlin. After demobilization we had a wonderful summer together, with a 21st birthday party for me at home in Kirkburton, where my father was now vicar, followed by a holiday in the south. We stayed with my Aunt Rosie and Uncle Reggie Tabuteau (now retired from the prison service), in order to attend the Bembridge Sailing Club ball, and our party included a neighbour by the name of Colgate. Martin promptly named the two daughters of the family 'The toothpaste queens'.

Martin went up to Pembroke and I to Trinity College, Cambridge, where I read Classics for two years and Theology for one. I spent too many hours on the sports fields and golf courses, and on the stage – in the Footlights and performing in Julian Slade's first musical *Bang goes the Meringue*. Out of the chorus of six, two of us became bishops and two deans, while another, Neil McGregor Wood, is a steward in Chichester. This was probably due to our amazing piano-playing chaplain Geoffrey Beaumont, who exercised a profound influence – he converted more young men at his gin parties (he spoke very directly) – than I have done in my sermons! Later on, after joining the Community of the Resurrection in Mirfield, he used to come and stay with us in Scarborough when he was on leave.

Many of the friends who shared these enjoyable years at Trinity, such as Tony Lloyd (later Lord Lloyd of Berwick), Douglas Hurd (later Foreign Secretary), Charles Willink (son of the master of Magdalene), John Pryke, John Polkinghorne (later master of Queen's College, Cambridge, before becoming a priest), Francis Chute, Christopher Luxmoore (later Bishop of Bermuda) and Patrick Appleford (the hymn-writer) were also committed Christians, and we would sit together in chapel for the Sunday Communion. In the week I sometimes went to King's for Evensong to hear the glorious sound of Borris Ord's choir. For my spiritual duties I saw Ken Carey, then Principal of Westcott House. After the Army I found it easier to develop my spiritual life and my vocation.

Having gained some maturity through National Service, I think we had a greater appreciation of university life and perhaps contributed to it more fully, even if we did not do so well in examinations. My friend Charles was the first Willink ever to get a mere second (too much bridge-playing in his last year), while I just scraped through in my Classics. I did manage a second in Theology, thanks largely to Harry Williams, who was the best teacher I ever had. His mind was so clear that you could follow his thinking as he spoke – a true gift of communication. I remember him once saying that, if they were Christians, it was extraordinary that some of the brilliant intellectuals on the high table were still saying the prayers their mothers taught them.

I suppose the real benefit of Cambridge was taking part in many and varied activities and mixing with anyone and everyone. I joined the Magpie and Stump Society and was able to develop my speaking and debating skills. The requirement was to say the opposite of what you meant, which gave one an ability to think on one's feet! During my first year I played rugby and cricket for the college, after which I became secretary of the Trinity Field Club, the body over-arching all sports apart from rowing. The president and secretary of the Field Club were empowered to award college colours to those who excelled in any sport for the college, which gave one many contacts. During my last two years I played golf, aiming for a blue but eventually becoming secretary of the Stymies, the second team. We played all the famous clubs round London and the seaside links in Norfolk and Suffolk, generally leaving the senate house at 6 o'clock on a Saturday morning. In my final year Christopher Lever, a good Trinity friend who just failed to make the side, kindly caddied for me. My opponent and I were all square at the turn when Christopher produced a bottle of champagne. This improved my golf but my affected my opponent to such an extent that he could hardly hit a shot. I won. Such was the gamesmanship between the two teams.

The next step, after three wonderful years at Trinity, was theological college. Christopher Luxmoore and Pat Appleford, who were also ordinands, told me that we would never do any work for the Lord if we stayed in Cambridge, so we must choose elsewhere. They opted for Chichester and told me to follow them when the time came. The Principal of Chichester was Dr John Moorman, the great Franciscan scholar and later Bishop of Ripon and an Anglican representative at Vatican II. He was also son-in-law to G. M. Trevelyan, our master at Trinity, and was to take part in my consecration in years to come. From the moment we met, he was a great influence on me, as was the chaplain, Jim Hannon. Thanks to my father's spiritual discipline I found the daily round of prayer, the Eucharist and offices, wholly congenial, and the lecturers interesting and educative. It was slightly easier for me than many of the older men as I had read Classics and Theology at university. I was able to continue at sport: cricket in the summer and hockey in the winter, in both of which the Principal participated and was no mean performer.

I shall never forget my first Sunday. It was the custom to take services in the surrounding churches, and I was sent out with the senior student Bill Hitchinson to Tangmere. We were met at the door by a great character, Miss Lillywhite, who was churchwarden, organist, choir (!), sacristan and verger.

She asked if I was taking the service and told me that as the canticle we would have the Nunc Dimittis. 'The Nunc Dimittis at Matins?' I queried. 'Yes,' she replied, 'but I do ring the changes in Advent.' She then turned to Bill and said, 'So you're preaching. You needn't if you don't want to, as we like everything short 'ere'! We had Tallis' festal responses, and during them she shrieked the response, which has a high note on 'and mercifully hear us when we call upon thee'. It was some time before I could sing the next versicle! We learned afterwards that the reason she liked brevity was because her cats had to be fed promptly at 11.30 a.m. I don't know what the cats did the next Sunday when we sent a student who was a ponderous theologian. His average time for sermons was 40 minutes!

I had learned the organ at school under Dr L. H. B. Reed, a great character who became organist of Christ Church Cathedral, Dublin, after Leatherhead because, so it was rumoured, the Guinness was cheaper over in Ireland. Apart from one piece by César Franck, I had been brought up on a German diet, so the French music I heard when I went into the cathedral at Chichester was new to me: it was the first movement of Widor's Fifth Symphony of which the famous Toccata is the last. I then met the person playing it, Anne Sheail, the assistant organist, and, as I have told, a friendship blossomed.

After Chichester came ordination in the London Diocese by Bishop William Wand, to whom I felt I owed some loyalty as he had awarded me the Monk scholarship. Our ordinands' retreat was held at the Royal Society of St Katharine in the east end, and we were ordained in St Paul's Cathedral. Olly (my friend from Elland days) and Anne both joined my family in the congregation. John Eastgate and I were assigned to St Peter's, Ealing, for our title under Father Henry Cooper, a good trainer of priests, who, as editor of the *St Raphael Quarterly*, gave me my first lessons in the healing ministry and taught me how to anoint with oil. John was put in charge of the uniformed organizations and I had the very active youth club.

My priest's retreat was spent in the Cowley Fathers' house in Westminster, and there were so many of us – one was John Habgood, later Archbishop of York – that I had to be billeted in the Deanery. I was most embarrassed (we were supposed to be in silence) when Dr Alan Don's manservant tried to ply me with the odd whisky each evening, thinking I was in need of some 'spiritual support'. We were duly ordained, and imagine my surprise when I found that Anne was sitting in the seat exactly behind mine, under the great dome of St Paul's Cathedral. Was it a 'prompting'? I had always said that I would go right through with my ordination before I thought of marriage. The thought came rather earlier than expected.

Anne and I gradually realized there was more to our friendship than music and sport, and our courtship, which had begun in my last year at college, was resumed after my ordination and became more serious. We used to meet on my days off, usually at Dorking North station, Anne coming up by train and I travelling down by car. There would follow a jaunt into Sussex, often to Chichester, with a picnic on the way. We began to pray about the future, as our love for each other deepened every time we met.

Chapter 2

Marriage and our move north from London to the Yorkshire Wolds

Some marriages are made in heaven. I believe ours was one, especially when we considered the difficulties we both faced on earth! There was a 16-year difference in our ages and, if truth be told, Anne was still bearing some scars from her unfortunate earlier experience. But we had both said our prayers and knew we were being called by God to pursue this course. I had seen my vicar and bishop, both of whom tried to dissuade me, but the latter eventually said that if I had fully decided, I should get on with it.

And so, on one of my days off, 18 July 1955, I arranged to meet Anne at Dorking North as usual. On the way south, we stopped at little Hardham church near Pulborough. My intention had been to ask her in Chichester Cathedral, but I couldn't wait that long! So I popped the question there and then. After a short silence, which seemed an eternity, Anne said a heartfelt 'Yes'. We had a joyful picnic lunch in a beautiful spot just below Whiteways on the Downs, then went into Bognor to buy the ring. Hawkey was so happy to learn of our engagement when we eventually reached Chichester, though we knew he must feel some apprehension at the impending loss of his assistant and housekeeper. He was 77 at the time.

Bishop Bell made Anne go to Somerset House and gain written proof that her first husband had died, which of course she did. Sadly, the great Dean of Chichester, Arthur Stuart Duncan-Jones, had passed away earlier in the year, so it fell to the Precentor, Rupert Browne-Wilkinson, to marry us. He and his wife very generously offered us their house, the Residentiary in Canon Lane, for our wedding reception. Imagine our surprise on our retirement 40 years later, when we moved into the Chantry next door.

We had a dinner party for family and friends in the Dolphin and Anchor Hotel opposite the cathedral on the eve of the wedding. My mother, Aunt Rosie, Nina and Helen – then aged 11 and on holiday from the Elmhurst Ballet School – were all there. We were married at 8.30 the following morning in order to have the choristers before they began their lessons. Alwyn Surplice had come over from Winchester to play the first part of the Nuptial Mass (though he found it hard, at that unearthly hour, to forgive my request of the Gigue fugue before the service!). Hawkey gave Anne away, and John Eastgate, my colleague at St Peter's, Ealing, was best man. Anne and I always revered the place at the altar rail where we first knelt to receive our Communion as man and wife. Hawkey played the second part of the service, including the Widor Toccata before it became popular, and Father Cooper gave the address. Anne and I left at noon for our honeymoon, driving westwards to Cornwall. The car broke down in Romsey but was repaired, fortunately, while we were enjoying our lunch. And so we arrived for our first night together, at the old Three Cups Hotel in Lyme Regis.

The next day we drove on to South Brent in Devon to see Uncle Rex and spend the night at nearby Holne Chase (where there was a power cut and we had to go to bed by candlelight!). The weekend saw us in Truro, and the rest of the fortnight was divided between the north and south coasts of Cornwall.

While staying in Carbis Bay the following Sunday, we attended the 8 a.m. celebration, and after the service the vicar asked if I was a priest. 'Yes,' I replied, 'and we are on our honeymoon.' He looked downcast. He was the Rural Dean with an interregnum to look after too, and the poor man had buried his wife only the day before. He wondered if I could possibly take the service at St Just that evening. What could I say? We duly drove to St Just for Evensong.

Those two weeks were memorable for their sheer joy, as our love deepened physically, spiritually and mentally. Anne took up golf so that we could always play together, and we explored as much of the coast as possible, walking north and south from Land's End, always keeping the sea in sight. We were sad to leave Cornwall as we set off for our new parish, St Andrew's, Uxbridge (with St Peter's), but received a great welcome when we arrived, on the evening of the church's Harvest Supper. The Bishop of Kensington, Cyril Eastaugh, had found a parish with accommodation for a married curate, a rarity in those days, though the 'house' was in fact the middle section of the converted vicarage, and not the best place in which to start a new life together. The family in residence was made up of late *and* early birds, and the older sister used to park her car under our window and not get round to running it into the garage until after 1 a.m. Anne told the vicar that unless the offending vehicle was put away earlier she would throw it over the hedge! Mercifully our relationships did not suffer. In any case, Anne and I were buoyed up by the deep happiness and sense of fulfilment our honeymoon had brought.

The vicar of St Andrew's, Father John Carr, lived with his rather frail mother and two sisters, the elder of whom was a chain-smoking social worker, and the younger (subsequently) an Anglican nun. His verve and sense of humour went down well with the many boys in the youth club who came from rough homes. I was expected to look after them on Sunday nights, when I was up against the blare of the new skiffle sound (rock and roll was yet to come!). In my second year, the vicar entrusted me with the parish magazine, a 'rub it out and do it again' affair, which I redesigned and renamed *The Fisherman* in honour of St Andrew and St Peter, our patrons. I wrote many of the features myself, including a humorous news slot called Pooh Corner. How could all this be paid for? Advertising was the obvious answer, and I trudged round every shop in the town during a heatwave, offering a quarter-, half- or full-page slot. From then on the magazine made a profit, much to the delight of our Scrooge-like treasurer.

We had two disappointments at St Andrew's. The first was that, although Anne was given scope to found and run a Young Wives' group, she was afforded little opportunity to use her musical talents. The organist had glue on his trousers and was very self-opinionated. (He did invite Anne to play at the 6.15 a.m. High Mass on Holy Days!) However, Hawkey was happy to have her back on two or three occasions ('Can't trust my new assistant'), including the enthronement of Bishop Roger Wilson who succeeded Bishop Bell in 1959. Roger had been my father's bishop in his later years and was a good friend. The *Church Times*' headline the following week read 'Magnificent music at Chichester', for Anne had been joined as usual by the trumpets and trombones of the Royal Marines.

The second disappointment was that the vicar did not like me staying away overnight, so the times we could drive down to Sussex and see Anne's parents were limited. I made sure later on that my curates could always get away for 24 hours. Father Carr did, however, train me well in the catholic faith of the Church of England and in all the ceremonial through which it is expressed. The High Mass was a high point of the week and I came to love the service of Benediction. I am grateful to him for this.

By this time it was becoming clear that we would not have children, which was a further blow. We had to rely heavily on God's grace to sustain us through this difficult time, and gradually began to accept that God could use our childlessness for his purposes. This was confirmed in our hearts and minds when we saw the way our work was to develop.

Towards the end of our three years at Uxbridge, I tried for the Chichester Diocese but the Archdeacon declined our request. Ironically, in our retirement we came to live in his very house! Another diocese we sounded out was Bath and Wells. During my post-ordination training I had researched the life of Bishop Thomas Ken, now mainly remembered for his beautiful morning and evening hymns. 'Who shall have Bath and Wells but the little man in black,' said Charles II of Thomas Ken, adding 'who refused to give poor Nellie a lodging.' I had handled Thomas Ken's New Testament in the library at Longleat, and his chalice and paten in Frome where he died. But our search in Bath and Wells was only to come to fruition much later on.

So we turned towards the north and wrote to a friend of my father's, Bishop Townley of Hull, who invited us up to stay. After considering a city church, we decided on a trio of country parishes on the Yorkshire Wolds and were duly summoned to Bishopthorpe for an interview with Archbishop Michael Ramsey. He sat us down in his drawing room, then in the medieval building, and told us he was sending us to Weaverthorpe, Helperthorpe and Luttons Ambo, relishing every syllable of the names. He added: 'And when you get there you will find you have a Rural Dean with a head shaped – er – er – rather like a boiled egg!' Six months later, when the Archbishop instituted me to the parish, Anne and I were placed on either side of him at the celebratory 'do' (as he called it) – a sit-down meal in the school. When the Rural Dean rose to speak, the Archbishop leaned back in his chair and murmured, 'And what did I tell you about your Rural Dean?' We were as taken by his sense of humour as his amazing memory.

The Rural Dean, George Wadge Thompson, presided over a happy ship, and he and his hard-working wife made us feel very welcome. Chapter meetings began with Holy Communion, followed by breakfast, after which the so-called 'shadow cabinet' (i.e. the wives) washed up and relaxed together while we had our meeting. These occasions were always something we looked forward to.

I was blessed with a set of six good churchwardens, who listened courteously to my suggestions and for the most part welcomed and helped them to fruition. The first task was to visit, visit, visit. Anne had bought a second-hand Triumph Mayflower in Uxbridge, which was useful to get to the furthest parts of the parish, though I also did a lot of walking round the lanes in the four villages served by the three churches. Weaverthorpe was a fine Norman church, but situated on a hill and thus rather difficult for the elderly. Helperthorpe and West Lutton were built by the great Victorian architect G. E. Street and paid for by Sir Tatton Sykes, the local landowner at Sledmere. They were designed for the catholic style of worship and contained (empty) vestment chests, which the Ladies' Guild in the parish and Anne kindly began to fill. We formed a choir of eight boys, two altos, a tenor and a bass at Weaverthorpe and robed them, and then recruited and robed 11 servers in the parish, with the full support of churchwardens and parishioners who raised the money. I managed to give each church at least one service every Sunday, though on festivals – with a Eucharist in each and an increasing number of communicants – it was a bit of a rush. By our final year, when the second-hand Triumph had been replaced by a beautiful red Riley 1.5 with leather seats (generously bought by Anne with the last of her savings), the journeys between churches had become rather speedier!

The Sledmere Festival, organized by the Vicar of Sledmere, James Seller, Anne and me, was a great occasion, remembered for years to come. We invited all the surrounding parishes to take part and had 150 in the choir (trained by Anne, naturally). James invited Archbishop Ramsey to preach, and at the end of Evensong we had a procession so lengthy that one end met the other at the chancel. James stayed rather long on the altar step at the end of the hymn and received a tap on the shoulder from the Archbishop who said, 'Do you think I ought to give the blessing?'

It was during this time that I began to be involved with the life of York Minster. I became a chaplain, which involved doing a day's duty in the summer, loitering with prayerful intent. The Dean, Eric Milner-White, was a saintly man, famous not only for his knowledge of stained glass but also for his beautiful private prayers, which were published under the title *My God, My Glory*. I shall never forget his reading of Hebrews 11/12 on All Saints' eve, especially the phrase 'Of whom the world was not worthy'. We came to love the Minster, which was to remain our cathedral for 25 years. We were prayed for, known about and loved by our beloved Archbishop, and under him I was able to read more widely and think more deeply. Our three years in a remote part of the Yorkshire Wolds, with a large number of 'characters' in the congregations, had taught me how to be a pastor, while Anne was certainly afforded opportunity to increase her sewing skills!

But then Archbishop Michael was appointed to Canterbury. At his farewell service, there was standing room only in Beverley Minster, a magnificent church which was to have significance for me in the future. Almost the whole diocese seemed to have turned out – people from the great conurbations of Hull and Middlesbrough, as well as York and Selby, and all the legion of villages and market towns. When we reached the front of the queue to utter our own grateful goodbye, Archbishop Michael immediately said, 'Ah, I've written a letter to you today. Mark well its contents.'

We didn't sleep that night.

The next day he left for Canterbury.

Chapter 3

By the seaside

The letter from Archbishop Michael contained the offer of the parish of St Martin-on-the-Hill, Scarborough, with encouragement to do something about the music and worship, and an injunction to 'get both feet' into the five schools and colleges nearby. It came as a shock, because I knew that this parish had always been staffed by senior men. Indeed, a senior churchman in the diocese wondered how I could possibly accept it. But there were five patrons – the Archbishop, the Dean of York, the archdeacon of the East Riding, the senior Canon Residentiary and the vicar of Hutton Buscel – all of whom I knew well. As Anne and I prayed, it seemed that if such people unanimously thought I ought to go, then God must be in it. So I accepted, feeling more than a little daunted by the huge task ahead.

The church was beautiful, a pre-Raphaelite museum, though I was determined it would be a museum in one sense only! It had been built in 1860–3 by G. F. Bodley, who invited his friends to help decorate: William Morris fashioned the sanctuary, while Philip Webb, Ford Maddox-Brown, Edward Burne-Jones and Spencer Stanhope were involved in painting the stained glass of every window and the pulpit. There was a lovely Lady Chapel and, to gladden Anne's heart (though in need of some restoration), a magnificent Henry Willis three-manual organ.

The programme on Sunday mornings consisted of 7 a.m. and 8 a.m. Holy Communion, 10.15 a.m. Matins (a large congregation) and 11.30 a.m. High Mass with full ceremonial (but only a small congregation because people were discouraged from receiving Communion so late in the morning). The afternoon began with a well-attended Sunday School at 2.30 p.m. and ended with 6.30 p.m. Evensong (solemn on all festivals). I also had to take a 9 a.m. Sunday service at the attached mission church once a month and, of course, daily Holy Communion and the daily offices at St Martin's. There seemed no prospect of a curate, and in fact I was to be two and a half years without one. It was clear I would have to give up all outside work, including the Minster, for the foreseeable future.

The new Archbishop was to be the Bishop of Bradford, Donald Coggan, an evangelical to whom (it is rumoured) the Dean said, 'Your Grace, if you come into my Minster you must come properly dressed.' Dean Eric appointed me as Canon's Marshall for the enthronement, which was a beautiful service with a fine sermon from the new Archbishop. He graciously came to institute me on St Martin's Day, by which time we had moved to our lovely new home, also built by Bodley, opposite the south-west corner of the church.

It is always a good idea to leave things as they are for the first year in a new job. So, rather than change anything in the running and worshipping life of the church, I set about the task of getting involved with the schools. As St Martin's School was an 'aided' church primary and junior school, it was easy to go in at least once a week to take assembly and teach a class. Like all church schools, it was over-subscribed, and the headteacher had a difficult job in sorting out the applicants.

Bramcote was an upmarket preparatory school which

prepared many boys for Winchester scholarships. It had a totally Christian ethos, and the whole school attended Matins every Sunday. The two joint headmasters, Jim Hornby and Frank Hamerton, invited me to teach once a week, and I happened to be there on the sad day when Colgate Palmolive took over Terry's (chocolates) of York. I asked the two Terry boys what this would mean for their father, to which they replied, 'Please sir, he'll have to work harder'! That was a prophetic word because Mr Terry and I never did have the game of golf we had hoped to arrange.

Scarborough College was a minor public school, with a fine headmaster, Denys Crew. I often enjoyed breakfast with him and his wife Gundred after celebrating Holy Communion in the school, and taught a class there on and off during my decade in the parish. The junior house head, David Blunt (son of the famous Bishop of Bradford, A. W. F. Blunt), was also my Reader and a good friend – he was borne away by Archbishop Coggan after a year or two to be his first Lay Chaplain.

The North Riding College of Education, a teacher-training establishment further up Filey road, was expertly presided over by Edna Madge. Like the headmasters, she was on the Parochial Church Council, and our verger, a great character who went by the descriptive name of Mr Shakeshaft, said to me on the way to my first PCC meeting, 'You want all your buttons polished before you go in there.' But Miss Madge became a good friend and supported my gradual reforms in the life of the church.

There were many hotels in the parish – mostly closed in the winter when we saw more of the owners and workers – 13 old people's homes and several blocks of flats, converted from the grand houses of Scarborough's Victorian heyday. (In a more leisurely age, whole households would drive up to the church in their carriages, be met by sidesmen in morning dress, and afterwards parade their fineries on the Esplanade.) By the end of my first year's visiting, I had found a large number of people who wanted to be confirmed, about 50 of whom were youngsters. They made a marvellous nucleus for a church youth group. Among other activities, they cleaned out and decorated the crypt and set up a coffee bar. The crypt became a centre for parish gatherings and eventually home to a flourishing art club.

The year 1963 was to be the church's centenary, and the leadership planned a large summer fête on Bramcote's playing fields, which was opened jointly by the popular singer Frankie Vaughan and Bessie Braddock, MP. (One ultra-conservative warden was not amused at this invitation to a forthright Labour politician, but at the end of the fête, happily gave her a kiss.) As for the spiritual side of the work, I invited 49 special preachers to speak on various aspects of Christian life and commitment, and arranged a mission with the Community of the Resurrection at Mirfield. Poor Anne was kept busy! She ran the house most cheerfully and efficiently, while her father, who had lived with us at Helperthorpe and moved with us to Scarborough, was doing wonders in the garden. But there was considerable extra work involved in offering so much hospitality. As it happened, the Mirfield father staying with us had just come back from Africa where there had been native boys to look after him. Anne was a little disconcerted by the habit he developed, on his daily return from Mass, of clapping his hands and demanding to know if his breakfast was ready.

The centenary appeal we launched was not a huge success. Though it paid for a new roof, the restoration of the fine organ had to be left to a future generation. However, the churchwardens and I did have some entertaining moments in the course of seeking contributions from parishioners. After being graciously received at one house, the owner showed us round every room, telling us the exact value of each of his galaxy of possessions and generally adding, 'Sotheby's won't get their 'ands on that!' He then allowed us ten minutes to explain why we had come. Three further requests were needed to elicit a small cheque. After he died, his chauffeur related how Sir went into the larder each evening, took out two eggs, weighed them, and put a cross on the heavier one – that was for him the next morning, the other doing for the housekeeper. She was eventually rewarded in his will, thanks only to the perseverance of the chauffeur.

Another set of characters was an ex-Romany family who had settled in Scarborough and owned most of the arcades on the seafront. All the womenfolk attended church faithfully according to Romany custom, while the men came only to funerals but were generous to a fault: after admiring the tie of one member of the clan, who promptly gave it to me, I realized I must not admire anything else!

It was Anne's initiative that led us into the healing ministry. Out of the centenary year at St Martin-on-the-Hill came the establishment of a Women's Fellowship under Anne's chairmanship. Joy Howard-Vyse, whom we knew from Yorkshire Wolds days, was invited to speak at an early meeting and told of the small prayer group she had formed to intercede for her brother who was dying of cancer. Gradually the group began to pray for many other sick people far and near, and found there was a remarkable change in them for the better.

Some of the Women's Fellowship asked us if they could form a similar group to pray for the people I named in the intercessions at the Eucharist, and the Prayer Guild came into being. After sharing news, including projects affecting the parish, we had a short service in the Lady Chapel. As time progressed, the Guild proved to be one of the mainstays of our life together. I was glad of my training by Henry Cooper in Ealing days, and made sure that some of my sermons were about the healing ministry of Jesus and the healing sacrament of anointing. This material proved useful for the first book I was to write.

Some time later, our beloved verger fell seriously ill and was admitted to hospital. His surgeon, a good Christian friend, rang me late on a Sunday night and suggested I come and visit that night as Mr Shakeshaft might not still be with us in the morning. It was nearly midnight as Anne and I set out with the oils of anointing. We found the patient in an oxygen tent, surrounded by medical equipment which made it a little difficult to get near him. I asked the nurse to draw the curtains and stay with us while we had the anointing, one of the most beautiful ministries offered by the Church. When we began the prayers, the verger was barely conscious but, after the anointing, he was able to mouth the words of the second 'Our Father'. At the end of the short service, the nurse and Anne drew back the curtains and, although it was by now nearly 2 a.m., some of the men on the other side of the ward were awake and sitting up. One of them called me over. ''Ere,' he said, 'summats 'appened be'ind them curtains.' The curtains had not been able to hide the grace of God from that rough Yorkshireman. He had discerned more than me, and I have never closed the curtains in ministering to patients since.

My Yorkshire friend proved to be a prophet, for the next day the sister on duty declared, 'The bad language seems to have cleared up overnight.' When the doctors did their rounds they found the verger's blood count normal, and in a fortnight he was back in church. He died of the same disease two years later, but during that period he was a powerful witness to the healing power of Christ. I believe our Lord healed him for our sakes and the parish's. It put a good injection of faith into our life and witness, and spurred us on to new efforts.

We decided to have a healing mission and booked the Revd George Bennett, Warden of Crowhurst Christian Healing Centre near Hastings, to conduct it. Nurtured in the Coventry blitz as a young priest and later in a hospital chaplaincy, he was a compelling and grace-filled teacher with a remarkable influence on the clergy and laity of my generation. His mission led to a great advance in the healing and spiritual life of our parish, and this was the first of many times I was to seek his help. I can still remember his opening address. 'The Holy Spirit is performing a remarkable work in our time: he is restoring the healing ministry to his Church.' It appeared that God was calling me to be one of those who would continue George's work, and this became more evident at my consecration and in my subsequent ministry. Meanwhile, I was asked by BBC Radio to do a teaching service on the Christian faith and chose 'Christian Healing' as the subject.

One of our regular congregation fell ill with cancer. Her son, a former MP for York, travelled up to Scarborough in a blizzard so he could be at her bedside as I performed the anointing. For most of her final three weeks she was remarkably lucid, and invited her many friends to come and say 'Au revoir', entertaining them with such wine and nibbles as she could get hold of. She died in great peace. Afterwards her son wrote to me, 'As I knelt at her bedside, I have never felt so near to God and all that was good in creation.' The son's name was Charles Longbottom, and he and his wife Anita became the firmest of friends to us from that moment on. Later he was to be chairman of Acorn.

The regular round of the healing Eucharist on Thursdays and the Prayer Guild on two evenings of the month continued, and I noticed that we began to do things a little better: the worship and singing of the hymns became more meaningful; the regular visiting by the clergy took on a new lease of life; conversations became deeper and there were more questions about the faith. The parish also became a happier place as fellowship among the congregation blossomed. It could all be traced to the healing dimension of the ministry, the devoted prayer of a small number of people, but above all to the merciful grace of God. I was always grateful to Anne for taking that initiative in her Women's Fellowship.

After two and a half years, Archbishop Coggan kindly gave me a curate. He was a nice, thoughtful, committed young man, but before ordination had been advised to break off his engagement to concentrate on the priesthood. His health began to suffer and he became very depressed. Anne and I ended up searching for him on the cliffs, before mercifully managing to return him safely to his parents. I later became godfather to his little boy, while Anne became godmother to the daughter of our second curate, who was the son of the local bank manager. The renewal of the parish really gained momentum with the next two curates. I had been in touch with my old theological college in Chichester, and after coming up to view the parish, Cheslyn Jones, the then Principal, wrote to me saying, 'I'm going to send you a "Thus saith the Lord" person.' That individual was John Simpson, and life would never be the same again! The son of a Middlesbrough engine driver, he turned out to be a most sensitive and hard-working priest, whose preaching had a depth which caught the attention of even the young. But he was also possessed of a great sense of humour: at staff-meeting breakfasts, when asked to report on parish visits, he would give the most graphic and hilarious descriptions of the people he had seen. Anne often nearly fell off her chair laughing, and things only became more riotous when the next curate John Manchester arrived in 1969. Like his namesake, he too had an enormous sense of fun, though underneath this lay a truly pastoral and caring heart. He has remained in his first parish of Old Malton Priory for over 30 years, a testimony to the love of his people and his love of them. John Simpson, on the other hand, after a memorable tour as youth chaplain to the Diocese of Bermuda, has settled in Australia where he was a much-loved chaplain to all three armed services in turn. In so-called retirement, he travels the world each year, spending six months in some parish and bringing it to life. Anne had a great influence on both Johns, and we have all kept in close touch.

By this time, I had become chaplain to the Futurist theatre which I used to visit at least one evening a week, getting to know the cast of the shows, which had leads like Harry Worth, Ken Dodd, the Bachelors, Mike Yarwood and Frankie Vaughan. Every couple of years the Black and White Minstrels, who had begun their life in Scarborough the year we arrived in the parish, would do a season in the town. Anne and I would throw a party for the cast and the dressers, either in our garden or round the piano if Geoffrey Beaumont (by this time a monk at Mirfield) happened to be staying. The boys and girls all loved him, and he could launch into any number they wanted to sing with consummate ease.

We used to have an annual showbusiness service, led by the artists. One year a piano accordionist was invited to play as the offering was being taken, much to the discomfort of one of our churchwardens. However, when the collection – from a very full congregation – turned out to be the largest we had had all summer, he remarked we should have more piano accordions! On another occasion, when the Russians had just marched into Hungary, the girls of the Black and White Minstrels asked if they could dance to 'The Rape of

Hungary'. I agreed since it was in tune with popular feeling at the time, and offered them the sacristy in which to change. Unfortunately I forgot to tell John Simpson, who went barging in and was horrified to see a group of lovely girls in varying degrees of undress. Yet another year the service was broadcast on *Songs of Praise*: none of us has ever forgotten John Boulter singing 'Were You There When They Crucified My Lord?'

As the Scarborough season was the longest time the Black and White Minstrels spent in one place, I had the opportunity to prepare many for confirmation. One year our High Mass was booked to be the first service to go out on Yorkshire Television, and it happened that five of the boys and girls had just been confirmed and were to receive their first Communion. Not to be outdone by ITV, the BBC sent along a reporter and a cameraman who chose to interview the head dancer, probably because she was a real bombshell. For his final question her handsome male interviewer, who may have fancied his chances, asked, 'But surely a young pretty girl like you doesn't go for this Christianity business?' She slew him with one of her smiles and replied, 'That's just where you are wrong: all my generation are searching, and many of us are finding the answer in Jesus Christ.' Cut! A senior priest wrote to me, 'That television clip was worth a thousand of your sermons.' I couldn't have agreed more.

The service went off well apart from one close shave at the beginning. The camera was going to pan out to sea, swing round to the church noticeboard to show the location and then focus on me, standing in the porch ready to give the welcome. Just as the countdown was about to start, two men in blue suits, one carrying a radio, appeared on my right saying, 'Oh Vicar, just a moment . . .'. I waved them off, but they persisted, 'Won't keep you a moment, Vicar!' At this point our wonderful verger (not long after his healing) shot out of the church and physically pushed the men away, just in time for me to say to the camera, 'Good morning. Welcome to the Church of St Martin-on-the-Hill, Scarborough . . .' The same two men were later filmed going up to receive Communion, one of them still clutching his radio. It proved to be a very meaningful service. I had rehearsed and timed my sermon in front of Anne the previous evening: she was always my mentor and a most loving critic.

We used our holidays from Scarborough gradually to 'golf' our way round the Scottish coast, stopping off regularly to see and walk in the beautiful countryside. On one break we stayed at Nairn where Harold Macmillan and his family used to holiday. We bumped into them one evening in their hotel. Harold Macmillan had been ill and I politely asked if he was feeling better. He replied most graciously in the affirmative. The next day, when we found ourselves in front of him and Lady Dorothy on the golf course, I sliced on to the beach so that we could wave them through and pass the time of day once more. Another holiday was spent in Golspie at the Links Hotel, which was next to a Wee Free chapel where the Sunday service began at 11 a.m. We noted the congregation coming out at 2 p.m. just as we were finishing lunch.

We had a slightly different kind of break from parish life when Anne was invited by Graham and Brenda Salmon to conduct a three-day course on the music of Elgar, Ireland and Bax in the Old Rectory, Fittleworth in West Sussex, which they had converted into a conference centre. We decided that I should begin each morning with a lecture on the composer of the day, while Anne would play some of his work in the session before lunch, always including a song or motet for those attending to sing. In the afternoon we would have an outing to a place associated with the composer, and in the evening play recordings of his music.

Anne was delighted to discover on visiting Brinkwells, the cottage near Fittleworth where Elgar wrote his cello concerto after the First World War, that the present owner of the house was none other than the widow of her folk-dancing instructor, Mr Rolt. Since Anne was in the party, Mrs Rolt got out Elgar's own gramophone and played one of his recordings. It made the day all the more special. We also visited John Ireland's last home, a converted windmill near the Sussex Downs, and felt that we could almost hear his piano concerto, inspired as it was by his love of this beautiful county. The third composer, Sir Arnold Bax, was well known to Anne, for he had often stayed with her and Hawkey in St Richard's Walk. (She once had had to do an emergency repair on his braces before a service!) It was no imposition to visit the White Horse in Storrington again, where we had been several times before we were married.

The course seemed to go well and was enjoyed by all. I was, however, a little disconcerted to find among the company Mary Gleaves, who had been companion to Bax and was left a lovely house by him, Widford in Storrington. I had read all the available books on each composer, but in my Bax lecture I several times had to add, 'Mary Gleaves will tell you much more about this than I can!'

In 1970, John Simpson left us for his second curacy. That same year, I called together my Roman Catholic, Methodist and Congregational colleagues in the South Cliff area of Scarborough, and we decided that our congregations would attend each church in turn once a quarter, sharing as much as possible in the service being offered by the home church. I believe the fellowship between the people in our part of the town encouraged others in the Scarborough Council of Churches (as it was then) to have more fellowship with neighbours of other denominations. It was one more step on the road to unity for which my generation of clergy had long been striving, though setbacks were to follow due to some of the decisions of our General Synod, and the differing conservative and liberal views in the Anglican Communion over the question of homosexuality.

The following summer, in an event that was to have far-reaching consequences for Anne and me, Archbishop Coggan was invited by the Council of Churches in Scarborough to conduct a mission to the town. The event was to take place at the open-air theatre, now derelict, but then a popular venue for Broadway shows such as *South Pacific* and *Call Me Madam*. I was in charge of the arrangements for the four Sunday evenings, and did my best to involve all the denominations: an ecumenical team conducted each service, backed by a choir composed of singers from every church. Dr Coggan's addresses undoubtedly contributed to the fact that the number attending increased each night.

On the third Sunday, he and his wife Jean asked if they could stay with us, previous invitations having been declined because of a heavy workload. It was a privilege to have them, and Anne was an excellent and welcoming hostess. Little did we know that we were being scrutinized! Some days later, as we walked Dr Coggan back to his car on the final evening of the mission, he suddenly turned to me and said, 'Are you doing anything tomorrow?' I thought I had better say, 'No, it's my day off' even though we had arranged to lunch with friends. He replied, 'Good, come to supper tomorrow evening. Shall we say 6.30?' I thanked him very much. A friend, Sister Mary, was staying with us and so I took her and Anne to the Station (now Royal) Hotel to have dinner while I went to Bishopthorpe.

Dr Coggan welcomed me, and we went out to the seat on the terrace overlooking the river. In fact it was the famous seat where Archbishop William Temple had sat with the Prime Minister, Stanley Baldwin, when a passing bargee, more used to seeing the Archbishop with trade union leaders and the like, shouted up: 'I see yer keeping better company today!' The Prime Minister wondered to which of them the remark was addressed. Well there we sat on 2 August 1971 and the Archbishop began talking about his plans for the diocese. Then out of the blue, I heard him say, 'And I wondered if you would join us as Bishop of Selby.' I was unprepared and utterly stunned. He continued, 'Perhaps you would say your prayers and write to me in due course.' From that moment, my sole recollection is of him walking me round the garden. I only came to when Jean greeted us at the door and told us that supper was ready. That meal together was the first of many which I, and of course Anne, were to enjoy with them.

Afterwards, I bade them a grateful farewell, promising to write, and went back to the Station Hotel to collect Anne and Sister Mary. My lips were sealed, apart from being told I could share everything with Anne, and so as I sat down, I traced the letter 'S' in front of her on the table. Such were Anne's perception and sensitivity that she immediately understood.

We prayed and considered for a few days, and then I wrote back to the Archbishop saying I was greatly honoured by the offer, it would be a privilege to serve the Church of God and him in this office, and that I gratefully and humbly accepted it. From then on, though excited by the prospect yet with a feeling of unworthiness for such a task, life became a little difficult. We both had to go on as though nothing had happened. I could not even tell my mother, who now lived just outside the parish. When my father died, she had moved to the Isle of Wight to be near her sister Rose, the widow of the prison governor in whose home we had often stayed. She was very happy there, but wanted to live nearer to us, and it was lovely from our point of view to have her so close. At this time she was not too well, and I longed to share our news, but kept my promise to the Archbishop. I also had to go on working and making plans for the future with my curate and readers, my churchwardens and PCC, with all the schools and various organizations, as though life was as normal. I was perplexed about one matter: the Council of Churches wanted to elect me as chairman for the ensuing year, so I rang the Archbishop about it. He was quite adamant that I must go ahead and be elected without any hint of what was to happen.

Once announced, it was all systems go, answering phone calls and the 400 letters we received, giving press interviews and doing radio and television slots. We fixed my resignation for the end of the year, and in fact Christmas Day was our final day of ministry. Our organist sadly fell ill a month before his fortieth anniversary, and it was Anne who had to play us out. The parish were very generous in what they said and what they gave us – Anne a beautiful present for our new home, me a silver crozier finely inscribed. I bought Anne a fur coat against the cold Yorkshire churches and she gave me my episcopal ring with its pale amethyst, the bishop's precious stone. My mother gave me my episcopal cross.

So ended the first major job that Anne and I had shared together. Our love for each other was paramount and we looked forward to our joint ministry becoming even closer in the knowledge that the Lord's grace would be sufficient for us, his strength being made perfect in our weakness.

Chapter 4

The early Selby years

Selby, a town on the east side of Yorkshire's old West Riding, is a few miles south of York. It was chosen as a Suffragan See by Archbishop William Temple because of its fine Norman abbey, which is similar to Durham Cathedral though on a slightly smaller scale. However, we found that the bishop did not live in Selby but in York, his job being to care for the city and its ten surrounding deaneries. Our new home was to be a pleasant house with a large garden, named Tollgarth (because it stood on the site of the original tollhouse) on the Tadcaster road.

We decided to move from Scarborough early in January 1972 to avoid any embarrassment to the parish that may have arisen if we had stayed on until the consecration. This had been fixed for the feast of the Conversion of St Paul (25 January), and was to be held in Beverley Minster since York Minster was undergoing massive repairs to its central tower and was virtually out of action, certainly for large services. The night before, we stayed at Bishopthorpe in the company of the Bishop-elect of Whitby, John Wates and his wife, and had a most enjoyable evening. Then it was a case of trying to sleep as best we could before being summoned to an early Matins and breakfast. The service was at 11 a.m. and had been masterminded by Paul Burbridge, Precentor of York Minster and later Dean of Norwich (fortunately for our nerves, there had been a rehearsal the day before). Anne was shown the eight seats she was allotted for herself and close family and friends.

Beverley Minster is a glorious edifice of cathedral proportions with symmetrical twin west towers, and was called 'the most beautiful medieval building in Europe' by Archbishop Cosmo Gordon Lang. It certainly pulled out all the stops for the service. John Wates had chosen the hymns, which happily included 'We Have a Gospel to Proclaim', while Anne had selected her favourite anthem *Expectans Expectavi* by Charles Wood. It was the first time the choir under Alan Spedding had sung it and they performed to perfection. My college principal, John Moorman, by now Bishop of Ripon, read the epistle, and I also chose the preacher, Stanley Linsley, Archdeacon of the East Riding and Chaplain to the Queen, who had been particularly kind and encouraging to us. He took his text from Acts 6, 'We will give ourselves to the ministry of the word and to prayer', and imagined a pilgrimage by St Hilda from Whitby to Beverley to encourage her pupil St John of Beverley – 'In fact two Johns today, John Yates and (Morris Henry St) John Maddocks'.

After the service the Archbishop said to Stanley, 'There was something wrong with the loudspeaker system, so I couldn't hear much of your sermon. Could I please see your manuscript?', to which Stanley replied, 'Sorry your Grace, I prayed it!' I had noticed on his way to the pulpit that he paused to pray at the St John of Beverley stone. At Communion, we took the Archbishop's hint to receive the sacrament with our wives, and Anne and I knelt side by side as we had done at our wedding. It was the crowning glory of a most moving service, during which, at the laying on of hands I had a powerful experience of the Holy Spirit's outpouring and the presence of the Church of the ages. Remarkably, this had also been experienced by many others in attendance, especially priests from my area of the diocese.

After the Archbishop's reception for the bishops and their wives, we went on to a parish hall in the town where Anne had organized refreshments – the large congregation had included a bus load from Scarborough, where John Manchester was now in charge, many friends and relations, and, touchingly, six of the Black and White Minstrels. We then had tea with a few close friends in the Beverley Arms and drove home to York. In the evening we laid on a dinner at the Chase Hotel for our family and Mark Green, Vicar of Bishopthorpe, who had put us up for a couple of weeks while we waited for our new house to be refurbished. So ended an utterly unforgettable day.

Archbishop Donald had told me to make a diary, and two days later we got started on our appointments. By 'we' I mean 'Anne and I' because she was my companion on all my travels round the diocese and, in the next job, round the country, unless she had an engagement of her own. Apparently this was rather unusual and began to be remarked upon. Even the diocesan professional critic told me that Anne at least got full marks for going everywhere with me! In fact it was a blessing for us to be able to pray together on our journeys. As we came to know the deaneries and the people, we were able to converse about the work and the tasks that needed to be done. Anne would talk to the women folk and musicians when she encountered them, which enlarged the ministry. Her occasional unavoidable absence was always noted: once when I emerged from the car alone, a Wolds churchwarden greeted me with, 'Evening Bishop. Ah sees tha's only doing 'alf a job tonight!' As more priests realized we worked together, they began praying for 'Morris and Anne our Bishop'!

Early on, we were very amusingly welcomed by Lionel

Griffith, a doyen of after-dinner speakers, at a lunch we gave for the 11 Rural Deans and the Archdeacon. In the afternoon, outlining my hopes and plans for the work ahead, I tried to express how grateful I would be for their help and advice. I requested three things: first, that they list the names of their clergy's wives and children so I could pray for them more closely; second, that Anne and I might spend three or four days in their deanery, worshipping and socializing (a suggestion that was gradually taken up over the next year or two); third, that we might visit each industrial undertaking in the parishes, including agricultural and manufacturing sites.

These industrial outings proved fascinating, if sometimes a little testing, for both of us. At one factory for instance, where pigs came in alive and went out as rashers of bacon, the manager asked if I would mind popping into the offal room where no VIP had gone before. I had a long chat with the two men who worked in it – one had served 17 years, the other 14 – and never before had they received an outside visit. Another outing was to lead to a new adventure for us: we went round two caravan manufacturing sites on the old Fulford air base where the prison now stands. In one factory, the standard of workmanship was geared to making affordable caravans, while in the other, professional craftsmen ensured that everything was handmade. After a year or two, we bought a beautiful caravan which we really enjoyed for a few years. We managed to pull it with a Morris Marina we had at the time. (Of course the diocese used to say as we drove up in the car, 'Here come Morris and Marina'.)

*   *   *

It was their experience of the outpouring of the Holy Spirit at my consecration that led some priests to invite us to their houses or parishes when there were cases of mystifying illness. The first to do so was the vicar of a country church who had five children: Kate, the middle one, had a problem with her legs and could hardly walk. When we arrived she was lying on the sofa in their living room, and as we all gathered round her for prayer, Anne and I laid on hands for her healing. Today she is a busy nurse and a mother, having fully recovered in only a week or two. However, soon afterwards, her father was driving out on to the main road when the front of his car was ripped apart by a passing lorry. The shock he suffered began to turn him blind. Again, he 'called for the elders of the church' and I invited him to come to our chapel at the top of our house to be anointed with the oil of healing. After the service, beautiful in its brevity and precision, I suggested that David should rest and allow the Lord to do his work. But he jumped up, saying, 'No, I don't want to lie down. I was going blind and now I can see', and then he danced all the way down the stairs ahead of us, in an act of thanksgiving to the Lord of the dance.

Thirty-five years later, David sent me an account of the event, which he had written shortly afterwards. It filled in many gaps. Since his final year at Oxford, he had suffered from iritis, a condition in which the infected eye is terribly swollen and affected by acute pain, also felt down the cheek and across the top of the head. Blood vessels tend to burst and flood the eye, which feels like the size of a golf ball. David suffered these attacks at fairly regular intervals and he was warned by his doctors that there was a fair chance he would go blind. Sometimes he was hospitalized and it always disrupted his work.

The attack in 1973 brought on by his car crash was really

serious and began to confirm his worst fears. David's words are significant.

> After the laying on of hands and anointing, the first surprise was the cessation of pain. It dropped off. It was as if I could have looked down and seen chunks of fractured pain lying around me where I knelt. I also rejoiced that through Christ my sin was forgiven, done away with, abolished. Nothing separated me from him. Like a previous experience on a dangerous hillside, it was as if the chapel walls had dropped away and we were held in a warm, powerful wind.

On being examined some years later, he was told that there was no sign of the 'craters' which iritis usually leaves in the eye. David had undergone a very real experience and this also had its effect on Anne and me. A new vista began to emerge as we prayed for guidance about Jesus' commission to preach and heal, a commission we believed confirmed by this event.

David, Anne and I decided to form a healing prayer fellowship. At first our monthly meetings consisted of those to whom we had ministered, but soon we opened the door to any individual or prayer group who wanted to join us. David acted as secretary and duplicated and sent out lists of prayer requests. After five years, he went to a larger parish and one of my Rural Deans, Maurice Pettitt, took over for the next 23 years, only retiring from the job at the age of 93! 'Bishop Morris' Healing Prayer Fellowship' still continues, thanks largely to the work and the enthusiasm of Leslie Stanbridge, once my colleague as Archdeacon of York. Leslie cemented things together by holding quarterly meetings at various churches, where the members had a talk, a time of intercession and meditation, a healing Eucharist and a picnic lunch. Recently the Prayer Fellowship has become an annual gathering, but we still receive the intercession leaflets on a regular basis.

This part of the work soon led to closer co-operation with the medical profession. Our own doctor, Walter Stockdale, and his wife Pauline were committed Christians, and members of St Michael le Belfrey, situated beside the Minster and presided over, for most of our time in York, by the famous priest David Watson. We already knew David – his wife Anne was to become a great friend of my Anne – and Walter always said he didn't know which of us was the more difficult patient! We both occasionally crossed the fine line of overworking.

I remember on one occasion Walter sitting down at our kitchen table, taking a stern look at me and asking to see my diary. He then proceeded to put a line through the whole of the next week. When I protested, he calmly replied, 'You haven't any work next week.' I asked him what he thought my boss would say about that! He countered that he would personally see the Archbishop to explain. Another time, Anne crossed the fine line and ended up confined to bed with an extremely bad cold. I rang Walter on the morning of Passion Sunday, a very full day, and asked if he would kindly call. He found her much worse than I had reported – in fact he had to stay with her for three hours to see her past the crisis point when pneumonia might have set in. I rushed home at once on hearing the news and have always been more than grateful to him for his skilful and prayerful ministry. He saved Anne's life that day. She had said, only a week or two before this, 'If one of us goes first, the most important fact is that we shall both be with Jesus.' I have always remembered this, and it has given me great comfort in my present condition as a widower.

Mercifully Anne had a good sleep and felt a little better

on the Monday. She was still not out of the woods but well enough for me to fulfil an engagement at St Michael le Belfrey on the Thursday, when I was to take the healing session in a course for 130 priests and leaders. Graham Cray, now Bishop of Maidstone, chaired the afternoon for David Watson, and before we began, asked if he and his colleagues could pray over me on Anne's behalf. I readily assented. To this day I believe that moment of prayer was the turning point in her illness. She soon threw off the virus, and I noted in my diary: 'Anne really is greatly loved everywhere – enquiries, gifts, good wishes and prayers have all been offered for her.' On Palm Sunday, I was able to bring her the sacrament and a palm cross from a confirmation and First Communion I had celebrated at Bishopthorpe parish church.

We had not really been very organized about days off. We knew that Donald and Jean Coggan worked most of the hours God sent them, and foolishly, apart from some gardening on a Saturday, had tried to do the same. From now on we made a real effort to have a free day each week, though we were not always successful (until Stuart Blanch came on the scene, of which more later). Playing golf wasn't really an option as we were living 40 miles from the Ganton course near Scarborough, so we tended to walk instead.

More fruitful was our decision to have two or three visits a year to the Graythwaite Manor Hotel in Grange-over-Sands, an excellent hotel set in its own grounds, with good food and comfortable beds. Not only was it on the estuary of the River Kent, looking across to Morecambe, but it made the whole Lake District accessible. Anne loved the Lakes and we both revelled in getting to know the area better. We also established a lasting relationship with the Blakemore family who owned the hotel, and it became a regular oasis for us over the years. For our holidays, we continued for the most part to go to Scotland, especially to the Galloway peninsula.

At home we forged ever closer links with doctors who had heard of our interest in the healing ministry. I began holding teaching sessions in St Olave's hall, just outside the city walls each year in November, which led to talks on the radio followed by phone-ins. In the summer we would meet for a whole day at a monastery or a convent. The healing ministry was becoming more resonant as the second melody in our work, and eventually it was to take over.

The summer of 1974 ushered in a major change, not just for us but for the whole Church of England. After nearly 14 years of devoted ministry and leadership as Archbishop of Canterbury, Michael Ramsey decided to retire. Who would succeed him? It took a little time for the decision to come through, which indicated that there were two or three names in the running. Eventually, despite being 64, which some thought too old, Donald Coggan, our Archbishop of York, was nominated. We all rejoiced for him and Jean, but it was a shattering blow: Anne had become very close to Jean, and I owed much to Donald and had felt it a great joy and privilege to work with him.

The enthronement was to take place in the New Year, but before December was out we received the dreadful news that Archdeacon Stanley Linsley, who had preached at my consecration in Beverley, had taken his own life after deep depression consequent upon his retirement. I suppose, like my own father, dear Stanley could not come to terms with life without his work and ministry. Donald returned to the Minster to preach at the funeral.

The enthronement was a magnificent occasion, executed beautifully by the cathedral chapter and community. Donald had kindly invited the three suffragans of his Archdiocese of York (Whitby, Selby and Hull) to be his chaplains, and we were quickly dubbed the 'three graces' by the Canterbury bishops! Interestingly, none of them knew Donald, and asked us what manner of man he was. We soon explained that, though undoubtedly an evangelical, at York his whole theology and sense of ceremonial had been enlarged. This tended to happen to all incumbents of the northern See, and Donald had had two of the great deans of York, Eric Milner-White and Alan Richardson, liturgiologist and theologian respectively, as his confidants and mentors. We also mentioned his sense of humour. I remember him whispering to me at one meeting, when someone was making a rather bitter and critical speech, 'He must have had two lemons for breakfast.' On another occasion we were stuck in a hold-up on the A1 as we tried to get to a meeting about diocesan boundaries. After a long wait, Donald looked up from his brief and said, 'I wonder how much of my diocese the good Bishop of Durham has given away so far?'

Anne and I returned to York to give our opinions at the Vacancy in See committee, pray for a right appointment and, in the meantime, keep the show on the road.

Chapter 5

The middle Selby years

There was quite an interval while the appointment wheels were turning: often in these matters, some refuse in order that the right man may be chosen. This was undoubtedly true in the case of Stuart Blanch, Bishop of Liverpool. He was a man of stature – an Old Testament scholar, an inspirational leader and teacher and, like his predecessors, devoted to prayer. He and Brenda gradually moved into Bishopthorpe Palace, and the enthronement ceremony in the Minster was a magnificent occasion. As Stuart expounded the passage from 2 Corinthians 4.5, 'We preach not ourselves but Jesus Christ as Lord, with ourselves as your servants for Jesus' sake', his humility shone through.

I have mentioned that Donald Coggan worked most of his waking hours. It was quite usual for him to catch the 7 a.m. train down to London, attend innumerable meetings and travel back to York in the late afternoon. On his way home from the station he might take in a couple of pastoral calls, perhaps to a sick or worried clergyman, then have a quick supper before disappearing to his study to catch up with the day's post and happenings. We were rather startled, therefore, when, at Stuart's first staff meeting, he said, 'Please don't bring me any morning engagements: I try to pray and read. I have a quiet time from 5.30 to 6.30 before I go out for the evening's work. Monday is my day off and here are my holiday dates for the next year.' We all wondered how long this would last now he was Archbishop of York, but it did, right through his tenure of office. However, the work was still done, even when there were a thousand letters to answer after a TV appearance.

⋆   ⋆   ⋆

One of the most important parts of a bishop's work was the laying on of hands in ordination and confirmation. The ordinations in the Minster were magnificent services, with crowds of people from the parishes present to support their ordinand or curate in prayer. The confirmations were important occasions for the parish, and I often took two or three a week. It was essential to be at the church in question half an hour beforehand since one was expected to sign all the baptism/confirmation cards and the devotional books being given to the candidates. Anne and I always felt that the reception afterwards for the candidates and their families was a vitally important occasion. Anne once told Audrey Walker, a Rural Dean's wife, 'I always try to learn the person's name, the names of the family and even their pets when visiting homes. People do need to be remembered. It makes such a difference.' Audrey was most impressed and resolved to do the same. I also worked hard at this, and more often than not, after thanking the ladies in the kitchen who had prepared the refreshments, we were the last to leave.

In later years, several candidates reminded us what we had said to them on these occasions: sometimes it had been a prophetic word. One also never knew what the Holy Spirit would do. I remember a girl candidate in Selby Abbey who had great difficulty walking up to me and even more kneeling down. After the laying on of hands, she got up and walked away normally. Her parents told me there had been a wonderful change in her.

Colleges and schools were always at the forefront during our deanery visits, or when we spent a day in a parish. Some of the independent schools had their own confirmations and we were able to meet not only the staff but also the children and their parents. The Minster Song School held its confirmation in the Minster which was always a joy. (I had been ordained with the headmaster, Bevan Wardrobe, who often invited us back for lunch.) At my first confirmation at St Peter's public school, whose foundation went back to the founding of the Minster in the seventh century, I was taken by surprise when the headmaster asked if I was likely to interrupt the service: apparently a bishop had stopped the boys one year in the middle of a hymn and told them to sing it faster. He later vouchsafed that his charges had become very lethargic, both in the classroom and on the games field, because February had been a gloomy month with continual overcast skies, often accompanied by bursts of rain. How much we owe to the sun!

It was in the chapel of St John's College in York, another of our educational establishments, that we first heard the hymn 'All My Hope on God is Founded', with its majestic tune 'Michael' by Herbert Howells. One of Howells' pupils, Geoffrey Coffin, was the assistant organist at the Minster, and he delighted in telling how his former teacher, on receiving Robert Bridges' magnificent words in the morning's post, had set them to music by the end of breakfast.

Around this time, Anne and I embarked on our first-ever visit to Ireland. The Church of Ireland had initiated the office of Warden of Healing in 1932, and its present holder, Stanley Baird, had made great progress in the work and been given a TV programme which showed him lecturing and conducting healing services. The healing ministry had its own church in Dublin, and in 1997 I was invited to speak at its annual conference.

Anne and I spent our first morning meeting and praying with the workers, and in the evening attended a healing service at St Ann's parish church, where a fine body of clergy was robed and ready to assist with the laying on of hands. Just as well, since the church was packed! I have always had cause to recall this service, since the illustration on the cover of my first book was drawn from a photograph of the ministry at the altar rail.

The following day I gave a lecture under the chairmanship of the Archbishop of Dublin, Henry McAdoo, 'a scholar pastor of rare ability', as he would be described in an obituary some 20 years later. I was very grateful for his sympathetic handling of the whole session, in which he allowed the questions to keep on coming but sensed the exact moment to bring things to a close with a prayer and his blessing.

The final day was in two parts. The morning was devoted to a session in one of the colleges with the clergy of the Dublin area. As usual, I gave some input and then asked them what advances they were making in their parishes. The ensuing discussion seemed to bring great encouragement, as everyone learned of the work already going on across the Dublin area, and we ended with a fervent commitment to pray for each other. I was encouraged by the morning, and adopted this model for other meetings of the same kind across Britain.

In the evening I had the privilege of preaching in St Patrick's Cathedral, and it was a joy for Anne and for me to hear some cathedral music again and to meet the cathedral clergy. When we left for home the next day, we felt we had learned a great deal.

★　　　★　　　★

I had found that the people who lived in the big houses in the parish often felt 'neglected in the ministrations', hence we made an effort to see them regularly. Lord Buckton, whose home was in Settrington, on the far edge of my area, had been Deputy Speaker of the House of Commons. He was a lonely man, so Anne used to spend the day with him as I went about my business visiting the clergy. A few years later, we celebrated our Ruby Wedding Anniversary in the home of his son and daughter-in-law, Richard and Virginia, who lived in the south. We also made great friends with his butler, Ireland, who had served in the Guards.

Another family were the Fitzalan-Howards. Martin was the younger brother of the Duke of Norfolk and was later to present Acorn with the Templeton Prize, while his wife Bridget was to become only the second High Steward of Selby Abbey since the Reformation. We also visited the Halifax family at Garrowby when I rededicated their refurbished chapel. The previous day the young daughter had been given an umbrella for her birthday, and as I began to sprinkle the holy water, she whispered to her grandmother, 'Granny, I think I'll put my umbrella up – it's starting to rain!'

Some of those I have mentioned were to take part in a family occasion at Selby Abbey. In the course of a trip to England a New Zealand cousin on my mother's side, Mary Titchener, had been keen to see Holy Trinity, Hampstead, the church built by our mutual great-grandfather Henry Sharpe on his return from missionary work on Wolfe Island, Canada. Two of its windows had been given by the parishioners in memory of Henry and his wife Sarah Hargrave Sharpe. On Mary's arrival at the church, however, she learned that it was under threat of demolition. I received an urgent telephone call and immediately rang up the vicar, who said that time was short but he was prepared to save the windows and give them to our family, provided they were removed in the next few days. Fortunately I managed to arrange for a glazier to transport them to the vaults of the Church Commissioners at Millbank. At this point Pat Womersley, who owned a printing house in Halifax and was chairman of the Selby Abbey Trust, said it would be good to have at least one window in the Abbey, and organized a lorry to bring them to York for inspection by Peter Gibson, Chief Executive of the York Glaziers Trust. It transpired that the glass had been painted by the nineteenth-century artist John Dudley Forsyth, and was well worth saving: two of Forsyth's windows were already in Selby Abbey, and Peter suggested that the one in memory of Sarah Sharpe, which depicted Christ with Mary Magdalene kneeling at his feet, and the figures of Anna and Phoebe on either side, should be placed in the north choir aisle. The original inscription was positioned underneath, together with a new one which included the Sharpe coat of arms and commemorated the day of its rededication by 'the present Bishop of Selby, a great grandson, on the feast of the Conversion of St Paul 1978' (the sixth anniversary of my consecration). Several members of my family who had subscribed towards the cost were present, including Nina and Helen. Pat Womersley, in one of his typically amusing letters, briefed us on the drill for the day:

> The dedication (of the window) will take the form of Holy Communion (1662). The chairman of the Selby Abbey Appeal [i.e. himself] will inflict on the congregation a large part of Acts 9, being the Epistle for the day. The High Steward of Selby Abbey will read the Gospel. The Bishop of Selby will give a short address.
>
> During the singing of one of the hymns the Bishop and his Corpus will lead the congregation to the North Quire Aisle in an informal procession: no doubt this will be orderly but it is to be hoped it will also be

dignified: the English have a genius for this. Then will follow the dedication, and the procession will return during the singing of the rest of the hymn. A collection will be taken for the Selby Abbey Trust.

Thereafter there will be a subscription lunch at the Londesborough Arms Hotel. This will cost £2.80 per head for thick soup, chicken and pud (*sic*!) and coffee, tips included but you pay for your own drinks. Please write a cheque for £2.80 per head in favour of the Londesborough Arms Hotel and let me have it.

After lunch Mr Peter Gibson, the chief executive of the York Glaziers Trust, will be Shanghai'ed into saying a few words about the quality of the window and why it fits so well into Selby Abbey.

At the beginning of 1978, we settled into a new home. We had been happy in Tollgarth, but suffragan bishops are not provided with gardeners, and though we both loved pottering about outside and found it good exercise, it was taking too much of our spare time. So we went to see Archbishop Stuart. His usual reply when I expressed a difficulty was, 'Problem? You know perfectly well it's insoluble by the time you bring it to me!', always said with a twinkle in his eye. However, he kindly listened to us and suggested that we look around for another house with a more manageable garden. When we found a delightful place in a small development in Upper Poppleton – the name being a gift to our friends who called us the Popples of Poppleton! – the diocese agreed the price and generously built on a study and secretary's office with the profit they made on the sale of Tollgarth. Meanwhile the owner sold us his very good carpets and curtains for only £1,000. All in all, it was a happy move.

★　　　★　　　★

The Lambeth Conference of 1978 was the first to be residential in the University of Kent at Canterbury. Normally suffragan bishops wouldn't attend, but this year six were invited and Stuart kindly nominated me as one of the two from the Northern Province. I would have the pleasure of Anne's company as there was to be a wives' conference during the first week, for which she had been asked by Jean Coggan to be organist/pianist. Anne was to stay with Hugh and Betty Albin at St Dunstan's where Hugh was Vicar – and the four of us were to form a lasting friendship as a result.

The Conference opened with a great service in the cathedral, and we processed in, not with a sonorous piece from the organ, but to a steel band demonstrating the universality of the Anglican Communion. Janani Luwum, Archbishop of Uganda, had just been martyred by Idi Amin, and we all wanted to applaud the Ugandan bishops as they processed in without him. After Donald Coggan, as Archbishop and Chairman of the conference, had preached, the steel band struck up once again, and I found Anne climbing on chairs to see how this unique musical sound was being created.

The bishops' conference was divided into three groups, and I was fortunate to be in that which had Desmond Tutu as chairman and Archbishop George Simms of Armagh as vice-chairman – both great men and complementary to each other. I shall always remember Desmond Tutu's opening words: 'Good evening, my friends, you are all such beautiful children because you are going to work so hard for me.' I got to know so many at the Conference over the three weeks, and the Albins kindly had a party for them – Africans, Australians, Americans, Canadians as well as those from Ireland and the UK. It was interesting to exchange ideas and experiences, and to pray together.

After worship and breakfast, the first session on spirituality was taken by Metropolitan Antony, and we all hung on his every word as he preached and prayed his address from the heart. A year later, when I was to interview him on the subject of prayer and medicine, I arrived a little early and was shown into the cathedral in Kensington. I began to walk round, stopping to gaze at the icons, and found myself transfixed in front of one. Just then, I was aware of the Archbishop's presence at my shoulder, and heard my voice saying, 'I began looking at this icon, and now it is looking at me.' 'Ah,' he replied, 'that is the essence of our spirituality.'

The final week of meditations was taken by my own chief, Stuart Blanch. Having been on retreat with the friars at Alnmouth on St Irenaeus' day, 28 June, he decided to base his talks on Irenaeus' great work, *Adversus Haereses*. His imaginary conversation between Irenaeus, who happened to be an 'observer' at the Conference, and himself, had us in hoots of laughter: 'Who are all these peculiarly dressed people walking about the campus?' Irenaeus asked, 'Do they know anything about theology?', and so on. This was followed by the brilliant teaching and meditation on the Old Testament for which he was famous. At the end of the week, many of the American bishops came over to me and said, 'Morris, your Archbishop is sure going to be the next Archbishop of Canterbury.' Sadly it was not to be.

There was one point that began to disturb me. I had spoken about the healing ministry to a good number of bishops and they had told me, in many cases, that it was a normal and regular part of the ministry in their provinces or dioceses. But no resolution about it had been produced. Mercifully there was an option open to us to propose a private member's motion. For the last weekend, Anne and I were staying with Fred and Mary Belcher – Fred had been at theological college with me – and we talked over the matter and together came up with a possible resolution, which I submitted the following week. It gained a sufficient majority to be put to the final session where it was passed unanimously as Resolution 8 of the Conference:

8. The Church's ministry of healing.
The Conference praises God for the renewal of the ministry of healing within the Churches in recent times and reaffirms:
1. that the healing of the sick in his Name is as much part of the proclamation of the Kingdom as the preaching of the good news of Jesus Christ;
2. that to neglect this aspect of ministry is to diminish our part in Christ's total redemptive activity;
3. that the ministry to the sick should be an essential element in any revision of the liturgy (see report of the Lambeth Conference of 1958, 2.92.)

This was at least a positive start in commending the ministry to every diocese. We were to do better in the 1988 Conference when I was a consultant to the Mission and Ministry section and invited to conduct some seminars. By that stage there had been ten more years for the ministry to develop.

The 1978 Conference has had its negative critics, but for many of us the opportunity to pray and study together, the fellowship, the stimulating lectures and the capable and efficient chairmanship of Archbishop Coggan of Canterbury made it a most positive experience. I was inspired to go home and begin writing my first book.

'Home', for the duration of our summer holiday at least, was a house Anne and I had purchased earlier in the year in Easingwold, north of York, in order to get on the 'property ladder'. I soon established a routine of spending two hours on the book before breakfast, and by the time we returned to Upper Poppleton, had all the biblical research done. After that I turned to it as often as my main work allowed, and was very grateful to Stuart for allowing me a month's sabbatical. Anne had always encouraged me to write a book, because, as she often remarked, I was constantly reading other people's manuscripts for publishers. She recorded in her diary: '10th January, 10 pm: Morris brought me the finished manuscript of his book, *The Christian Healing Ministry* and is going to dedicate it to me.' Disappointingly, my publisher, SPCK, had to give priority to the ASB (Alternative Service Book) and *The Christian Healing Ministry* was not published until January 1981. The chief editor was not very hopeful about its sale! However, SPCK had to run three reprints in the first year and has kept it in print to this day. Brian Frost, who helped me with Part 3, said prophetically after reading the manuscript, 'Morris, wouldn't it be exciting if you've written a bestseller?' It seems still to be looked upon as the standard work on the subject, even after nearly 30 years, though many good books have been written since. Others who read the manuscript and offered valuable suggestions were David Watson, Geoffrey Hunter (also a priest in York Diocese), Professor George Hudson in the Sheffield University Faculty of Medicine, and Archbishop Stuart himself, who contributed a most gracious foreword, in which he quoted Resolution 8 of the 1978 Lambeth Conference. In fact very many people, to whom or with whom I had ministered or whose writings had helped me, contributed to the book's formation, and I was extremely grateful to my hard-working secretary, June Hall, who typed the whole manuscript and, even after we left York, continued to type up all my other books.

*   *   *

When John Yates and I were consecrated, we found that our predecessors had been on so many diocesan committees that they had spent three and a half days in York each week. We decided that if we were to be pastoral bishops, something had to be done. We resigned from every diocesan committee apart from the pastoral one, which only left us with the occasional meeting of the Archbishop's Council and the Diocesan Synod, in addition to the monthly staff meetings, which were essential.

I also tried to limit my involvement with organizations outside the diocese, but took seriously my appointment (by Archbishop Coggan) to the Churches' Council for Health and Healing (CCHH), which met at St Marylebone parish church in London. All the Royal Colleges of Medicine, the BMA, all the Churches, the Quakers and the Salvation Army were represented on the Council, which had been founded by Archbishop William Temple. I served as co-chairman with Dr Kenneth Leese (a Methodist GP) for seven years and as chairman for three more.

The CCHH was a large, rather unwieldy body. Its greatest triumph, when Brian Frost was secretary, was to organize 'Health for the Eighties', the first national conference for the Churches with the medical and healing organizations. We met at Swanwick in 1981. Our keynote speaker was Dr Sidney Evans, Dean of Salisbury, our residential theologian was Professor David Jenkins who later became Bishop of Durham, and the chaplain to the conference was Stephen Verney, of *Fire in Coventry* fame, who was Bishop of Repton. The conference achieved its purpose: it brought together all the organizations and personalities at work in the health and healing movement and made us aware of each other; this greatly helped our working together, it stimulated the thinking and prayer movement, and it proved to be the launching pad and inspiration of future initiatives and combined enterprises. Much of its success was due to the hard work of preparation put in by Brian Frost and his colleague Peter Smith.

Kenneth and I shared the chairing of the sessions and I shall never forget the final session when I was presiding: David Jenkins, in summing up the conference, was so very moved by the truth of what he was saying, that he broke down. I allowed the ensuing silence to run its course, and those precious moments had a great influence on everyone. Stephen Verney wrote a prophetic letter to us afterwards:

> I think that under the loving auspices of you and Anne, something is coming to birth of very great importance to us all. A community of people who are being drawn into a new understanding of healing and health. We are coming 'to understand with all the saints what is the height and depth and length and breadth'. It was a great conference, and I am sure it will bear fruit in lots of people's lives.

A few years later Anne and I founded Acorn and I became the Archbishops' adviser on health and healing.

Chapter 6

Later years in York and Selby

The late 1970s and early 1980s saw us much involved in planning for an industrial chaplaincy to the massive new Selby coalfield, and we were pleased to be able to appoint a chaplain two years before the field was in full production. The appointment had not come easily. To his credit, Arthur Scargill, acting for the National Union of Mineworkers (NUM), had been immediately supportive of the scheme, but Mike Eaton, who was head of the coalfield development, took more convincing (Archbishop Stuart helped win him and the management over), and I had to hold six meetings with the local churches before their approval was finally secured.

The ceremony for the opening of the coalfield by the Duchess of Kent had actually taken place back in 1976. After the Duchess's opening words, I said prayers and then walked through the crowds with Joe Gormley, the retiring president of the NUM, who received a tremendous cheer from the miners. At the lunch that followed, Anthony Wedgwood Benn, then Minister of Fuel and Power, entertained the Duchess at the top table. Arthur Scargill, who was seated some way down, was of a mind to converse with her Royal Highness too, and when Tony Benn rose to introduce him, sat down on the vacated chair and stayed talking to the Duchess for some time. Eventually Tony Benn had to ask for his seat back!

We had a high-powered monitoring committee for the chaplaincy, which also acted as a support group for the chaplain. Fortunately, we were able to secure the services of Gwynne Richardson who had been chaplain to the Northumberland coalfields, and we attached him to the Brayton team ministry just outside Selby. He did a wonderful job with the miners and management: both were represented on the committee and gave him their strong support, professing that they had never worked in such a happy mine before. All our hard work seemed worthwhile.

Meanwhile, the appeal for Selby Abbey was going strong. The contralto Janet Baker, who in her young days had been a chorister at the Church of the Holy Redeemer in York, gave a memorable performance in the Abbey to raise funds, and afterwards Miles Fitzalan-Howard (shortly to become Duke of Norfolk) kindly asked many of us back for supper at his country house, Carlton Towers. Anne and I were fortunate enough to be seated at table with him and his wife, alongside Janet Baker and her husband. Anne was thrilled to have a 'musical' conversation with Janet, and we were interested to learn that her husband always tried to come with her so that he could drive her home after a performance. She liked her own bed!

Another concert was given by the Kings' Singers, one of whom hailed from Poppleton, and supper on this occasion was at historic Bramham Park, the Lane Fox family being our hosts. We drove there in a blizzard and only managed to return home in the small hours with great difficulty, being hindered by icy roads. Yet another event in the Abbey, when the weather was rather more temperate, was very special: the Monks of Ampleforth came to sing Vespers, and Cardinal Basil Hume, once their Abbot but now Archbishop of Westminster, was the preacher. His fine, hopeful sermon on unity was prefaced by the remark that he felt himself to be among friends, one of whom was 'his old friend, Bishop Maddocks'. I felt very embarrassed with both my boss and colleagues present.

On the Sunday following this event, the two of us set off early to Catterick for the Royal Signals Association in the presence of its patron, Princess Anne. I preached on Ephesians 6, 'Put on the whole armour of God', which gave rise to much talk afterwards. Anne was enthusiastically escorted by the senior officers and introduced to Princess Anne who wanted to know about our ministry, while I was presented with a Royal Signals tie because I had been a member of the regiment. We were both won over by the Princess. Our socializing continued the following day at the Mansion House in London with the Lord Mayor's annual dinner to bishops and wives, the last before Donald Coggan's retirement as Archbishop of Canterbury. Donald's great speech was worthy of the occasion and was warmly applauded. He had accomplished so much in his five short years at the helm, including his 'Call to the Nation' in 1975, which provoked a great response from the general public though it was poorly supported by his fellow bishops. He will be remembered for his utter goodness and openness, his fearlessness in speaking out, his prayerful and holy life, the commitment he brought to his work – and his sense of humour.

* * *

Holy Week in one of our last years in York was memorable. On Palm Sunday there was the usual confirmation and First Communion at Bishopthorpe. We tried to have some time off as usual on Monday, but the telephone rang continually for a large part of the day. I had a strong feeling on the Tuesday that I must go to the hospital, and there I met our Vicar, Arthur West, who was visiting his wife Nora. She was quite ill, and while Arthur clasped her hands, I laid on hands in prayer. She later told me she knew she was healed from that moment. As usual, Anne had been praying at home while I was out.

Maundy Thursday was a special day in many ways. I had the joy of celebrating the Chrism Mass with the renewal of priestly vows in the Minster. Ronald Jasper, the Dean, preached, and three of my priests, David Johnson, Jack Taylor and Gordon O'Loughlin, were the deacons of the oils. It was the first such service to be held in York Minster since the Reformation. On Good Friday evening, after I had preached on the Suffering Servant to a packed Minster, the Archbishop, David Watson and Martin Fitzalan-Howard came up and said that their hearts had been 'strangely warmed'. On Easter Eve I celebrated the Paschal liturgy in Pocklington church, once more with a packed congregation.

And so the year went on, but I had time to note, 'My darling Anne grows more beautiful, spiritually and physically in her looks each day.' I also recalled how she had played the organ at services at which five successive Primates of All England had been present – Lang, Temple, Fisher, Ramsey and Coggan. But she was equally at home playing for the parish churches. On one occasion, when the excellent worship was borne along by Anne's masterly touch and stimulus to the singing, everyone was in raptures of joy about the service. That day she preached a much better sermon than the preacher!

Anne and I always celebrated anniversaries in style, and 1980 saw both the Silver Jubilee of my priesthood on Trinity Sunday and our Silver Wedding. I marked the former by celebrating the Eucharist and confirming 50 candidates at the Abbey church in Selby, and at the reception afterwards five of the adult candidates from the previous year wheeled in a huge cake with 25 candles. With Anne's help, they were extinguished in one breath. It was a wonderful day, and we drove home singing.

We marked our Silver Wedding, first of all, by selling our house in Easingwold and buying a cottage in Oving Road in Chichester. We were there to celebrate our anniversary in September at a dinner party with some friends in the Dolphin and Anchor, after which they came to inspect the cottage and 'christen' it with champagne.

The following day we were given a party by Anne's family at her cousin's house in Aldershot, after picking up a new British Leyland Princess – yellow of course for Anne! – from the Church Commissioners' garage. The day after, my side of the family took us to a good hostelry near Haslemere, which had glorious views of Chanctonbury.

The year 1981 saw the publication – at last – of *The Christian Healing Ministry*. The Yorkshire press and Yorkshire Television responded at once and we went to Leeds to film for the latter. I was interviewed by our TV adviser, Margaret Cundiff – who was subsequently to be ordained and write several books herself – and produced by Graham Watts. It all came out right first time, and over lunch we told them about our projected home of healing for the north, Spennithorne Hall in Wensleydale, which was now in an advanced stage of planning and preparation.

More interviews took place in the south. We were in Chichester Cathedral for the anniversary of my consecration, then spent the night in Kent at Burrswood, which had been a run-down mansion when it was purchased in faith by Dorothy Kerin in 1948 to develop into a Christian home of healing. Burrswood was to feature largely in our lives in years to come. The next day we travelled down to Dover to film seven programmes on the trot. When the producer, John Barton, told me he liked my straight and simple answers to the interviewer's questions, I warmed to him, and this must have shown in the filming for we got through without any retakes being necessary. It was a bonus that the cameramen were so interested and quizzed me about some of the things I had said. After another stopover at Burrswood we went up to London to be interviewed by Radio Medway, Radio London and London Bible College, and afterwards signed books at SPCK.

The official day of publication was 29 January, and the afternoon saw us sitting side by side as usual for a signing at the SPCK shop in York. Fifty copies had already been ordered by people in advance, and in fact we sold 130. There was a queue throughout the afternoon, and it was lovely to be able to talk to so many well-wishers and friends. Later that week we drove down to Sheffield to thank Professor George Hudson of the Faculty of Medicine at the university who had read the manuscript before writing this commendation of the book:

> I think this scholarly work will be well received. The fact that it takes so broad a view of health and covers so many trends and developments in this area will make it a most useful book for all who are interested in the interface between religion and medicine.

We gave him a cross made from the oak in the tower of York Minster.

Other requests for interviews sadly had to be turned down owing to pressure of work in the diocese, but we had two interesting phone calls in March. The first was from Michael Marshall, Bishop of Woolwich, to say how 'excellent' he had found *The Christian Healing Ministry* and that he was already using it with his junior clergy as a Lent study book. He wanted to meet and talk, and eventually we were to see a good deal of each other. The other call was from SPCK to let me know that a second impression had been printed, and that half had already been sold. Later on at Burrswood I met Dr Martin Israel for the first time. I could see that his brilliance was cloaked by a quiet and gracious manner, and was greatly encouraged when he told me my book was the best on the subject to date.

In the meantime, much work had been done on Spennithorne Hall, our northern home of healing. We had formed a North of England Christian Healing Trust to finance and run it, and I had been chairman for two years before John Harris-Douglas took over. Pam Birdsall and her daughter Cubsie, having bravely sold their own house in Bramham, agreed to live in the Hall for the winter (a very bad one, of which more shortly) where, indefatigable and full of faith, they dealt with countless burst pipes before the eventual opening on Easter Monday 1982. Archbishop Stuart Blanch came to bless the building, surrounded by a large crowd of workers and supporters. At my suggestion, he spoke on James 5.13–15, and later, with a twinkle in his eye and quoting Martin Luther, asked why I had proposed a text from an 'epistle of straw'. After the ceremonies, David Young, the Bishop of Ripon, and I planted an oak sapling which had kindly been donated by Burrswood. And so came to fruition a vision which had been given to Anne and me and the members of our healing prayer fellowship many years earlier.

On one of our visits to London we were charmed to hear the young organist, Catherine Ennis, play the first movement of Widor's Fifth Symphony, the piece of music that had drawn Anne and me together. At a later date, one of Anne's ex-pupils, David Graebe, took us to Lancing College to hear Catherine give a performance of the Poulenc Organ Concerto. When we went to congratulate her afterwards she said to Anne, 'Golly, if I'd known you were here I wouldn't have played it!' Catherine, at the time of writing, is assistant organist at Christ Church Cathedral, Oxford, only the third woman to hold such a post after Anne.

To end the year I preached in Selby Abbey at the midnight Eucharist, which was broadcast by the BBC. Little did we think, as we welcomed in 1982, that by Twelfth Night Selby would be involved in near disaster.

⋆   ⋆   ⋆

January began with excessive snowfalls in the Yorkshire Dales. By the 4th, the River Ouse had risen 16 feet above normal, and the historic town of Boroughbridge in the heart of the county was experiencing its worst flooding in living memory. The next morning, York itself began to suffer, and soldiers and police worked throughout the day to help those in difficulties. The river was even rising up the roads behind our house in Poppleton! Selby was next down the river, and a whole-scale evacuation had to be carried out there. Anne and I offered what support we could by ringing all the clergy affected.

By the 9th, the water had gone down a little and we managed to get to Selby, to find that the Abbey and surrounding area had escaped by three inches. We met the chief executive and discussed an appeal for the town, which was launched a day or two later. (Michael Turnbull, at that time head of the Church Army and later to be Bishop of Rochester and Durham, had rung the day before to offer £1,000, as had Bishop and Mrs John Taylor of St Albans.) After touring the army units and watching numerous rescue operations, we visited St Francis' church, Thorpe Willoughby, which was being used as a hostel by people made homeless by the floods. The poor souls faced weeks of drying out their houses.

At this point, there were no roads open at all in Wales, while the temperature in Scotland was −27°C. In fact, the day after our visit the flooded centre of Selby froze, complicating things even further. The telephone rang all evening on our return home, with donations for the appeal.

Gradually life began to return to normal, and the end of the month saw the tenth anniversary of my consecration. After a joyful Eucharist at Goodmanham, one of the most ancient religious sites in the country, we went on to South Cave near Beverley to stay with Dr Storrs-Fox and his wife. He had been a pioneer – indeed, originally almost a lone voice – in promoting the Christian healing ministry in the diocese. That evening he took us to Beverley Minster, where Anne and I had memorably knelt side by side at the altar rail a decade earlier. To Anne's delight Alan Spedding was again in charge of the music at this Eucharist of Thanksgiving, and his fine choir sang the same anthem, *Expectans Expectavi*, before he played Bach's St Anne Fugue in Anne's honour. I preached on Acts 9.17, because of the connection with St Paul, both in ordination and consecration, and we all had a most enjoyable time over supper together afterwards. Anne was to be honoured again shortly afterwards, when as a guest of the York Musical Society, Dr Francis Jackson described her as a 'grand daughter' of Widor. Of course in pupillage terms she was. A few days later she began rehearsing the Mount School Girls' Choir for the Women's World Day of Prayer, and in March, with only the nave small organ, she and the choir led a packed York Minster in some vibrant hymn singing. I noted that Anne was still the calm and professional musician she had always been, and Stuart Blanch made a similar comment to me the following day.

★   ★   ★

As I related in an earlier chapter, I was not unfamiliar with the inside of prisons, and while in York, Anne and I had the chance to develop a prison ministry. On one occasion when I was celebrating the Sunday Eucharist at Armley gaol in Leeds, I was impressed by the hearty hymn singing and the deep reverence of the servers in their clean white albs. Afterwards I remarked on a very searching picture of Jesus on the cross. The chaplain told me it was by a prisoner, a hardened criminal, who had suddenly asked for a canvas, paint and brushes, though he had never painted before. His request was granted and the next day he got to work, refusing to stop even for meals, until late in the evening he lay back exhausted and had to be lifted on to his bed. He told the warder, 'I've offered my life to Jesus and I believe.' And though the warder laughed, time proved that he was indeed a changed man.

At a confirmation ceremony at Askham Grange, the women's prison not far from York, we enjoyed speaking with those who had taken part in the service. After a while, the governor came and asked if I knew where Anne was. I didn't. The governor noticed that one of the prisoners – a lifer – was missing and became alarmed. She began a search of the grounds and was greatly relieved when we found Anne and the missing woman deep in conversation about music, the passion of the prisoner's life as well as Anne's. How music crosses all divides!

We were also able to minister to the 'outcast and forgotten' at home. Like all parish priests, we received a procession of tramps, and one, whom we named Toofey (he lisped through a wide gap between his teeth), had an encyclopaedic knowledge of vicarages across England. Anne gave him a cooked meal every day and lodging through a bad winter down in the cellar boiler room, the warmest place in the house. Sadly, years later, Toofey was knocked down and killed on the road. A pottery firm owner, a publican, a bishop and of course Anne formed the congregation at his funeral.

Whit Monday 1982 saw the memorable visitation of Pope John Paul II, who arrived in his yellow helicopter on York racecourse. We had assembled early and were parked alongside the Duke of Norfolk, who produced a clothes brush and said, 'You brush me and I'll brush you!' Lined up in serried ranks, Anne and I were placed with the Bishop of Leeds immediately opposite the Pope. He had chosen the sacrament of matrimony as the theme of his visit to York, and Anne and I had the very great privilege of having our vows renewed by the incumbent of the chair of St Peter. We were able to look into his eyes, which often looked into ours. It was a great day, both for us personally and for the city.

Around this time Stuart suggested that Anne and I went to see him. He had noted that we were both under some tension between the normal part of our work and the continuing requests to speak about the healing ministry outside the diocese. Re-reading my book, he had kindly commented that he thought it was the best thing I had done, but wondered if it had led to an overload of work. As we drove to Bishopthorpe, Anne admitted that she still felt some of the stress she had been under during a visit to Burrswood earlier in the spring. I myself was longing for a summer holiday. Stuart was very understanding and proposed an immediate sabbatical 'to sort yourselves out', suggesting we contact John Bickersteth, Bishop of Bath and Wells, on the way to Chichester to see if there was any opportunity of working from his diocese. He also told us that Bob Runcie, as Archbishop of Canterbury, was contemplating the idea of some episcopal supervision of the burgeoning healing ministry.

On 1 August we set off, and our meeting with John Bickersteth in Wells the next day happened to coincide with the eleventh anniversary of Donald Coggan asking me to become Bishop of Selby. We discussed how Anne and I could tackle a nationwide ministry while I served the diocese part-time in my current role. John was very positive and agreed to call up several contacts regarding expenses and housing. I promised to go to the Pensions Board to see if my pension would still be secure under these new circumstances. A long walk around the cathedral and palace precincts, followed by Evensong beautifully sung by the Wells choir, completed a very hopeful day.

The Feast of the Transfiguration on 6 August brought one more day of work en route to Sussex before some real leisure. In the course of speaking at the Glastonbury Christian Festival, we met Lord (Raymond) Hylton, a Roman Catholic and founder of the Ammerdown Centre, a Christian community dedicated to peace, reconciliation and renewal located in the former stable block of his home, Ammerdown House. We struck up a friendship, and only a few months later Anne and I were to travel down to Ammerdown to invite him to be one of our first Trustees.

From Glastonbury we ambled towards Chichester, staying at the Wessex in Winchester to enjoy Sunday services in the cathedral, before stopping off near East Marden. There we were treated to the sight of several species of butterflies – brimstone, fritillary, tortoiseshell, peacock, meadow brown and red admiral – dancing over a clump of thistles in the sunlight. And so to Chichester to spend a couple of nights with Ron and Cicely Small (a great friend of Hawkey's in latter days when he lived at Hurstpierpoint, where he had given Anne all his music), in order to get the cottage ready for our stay. We went out to the Downs each day to unwind and began to notice things again: there was an enormous variety of wild flowers, and Anne remembered most of their names from her early life at Bignor. Around this time, I was thrilled to receive a letter from Dr Moses Tay telling me that my book was being sold in Singapore.

We began to read to each other in the evenings, something we had done on and off for years. Having completed the novels of Jane Austen, we had great fun with *Watership Down*, imitating the rabbits as they conversed with one another, and then began Mervyn Stockwood's autobiography, *Chanctonbury Ring*. We found it interesting to learn that he never took any big decision without walking on the Downs to the Ring, so a few days later we did the same. Anne was ahead of me (as often, in many ways!) and reached the Ring first, just in time to see a calf being born. Turning round, she said, 'New life'. It was prophetic. In another happy coincidence, that evening's broadcast of the Proms featured the Piano Concerto by John Ireland who lived opposite Chanctonbury Ring.

Our next port of call was a flat at the Crowhurst Christian Healing Centre, where we were lovingly looked after by the community. Here we enjoyed walks on Beachy Head and down to Burlington Gap, and trips to places like Burrswood and Chartwell, where we were inspired by Churchill's view over a vast extent of the Kent Weald. No wonder he was far seeing! While we were at Crowhurst, Dom Robert Petitpierre OSB (editor of the 1972 Church of England report on exorcism) came to stay. He had a remarkable gift of spiritual knowledge. When we visited a church with him, he paused at the chancel step and said, 'There is an eight-foot drop below this – perhaps the old Saxon church.' In another section he stopped and announced, 'This needs cleaning up', said a prayer and blessed it in the name of the Trinity. He went through the same procedure at a yew tree outside, saying there had been 'something' there. He called committees 'A

83

way of negating personal responsibility' and thought that they were the work of the devil!

My cousin Helen, who was working through a very difficult time in her life, joined us in the flat at Crowhurst. We had a soft spot for Helen and her brother John, whom I was privileged to marry to Mary-Margaret, and were to see more of them all in retirement. In the evenings we sometimes went badger viewing with our gracious hosts, the warden David Payne and his wife Anne. Like George Bennett before them, they lived in 'Godfrey's', named after Godfrey Mowat, another pioneer in the Christian healing ministry, who was blind. George used to assist Godfrey in the regular healing services at Holy Trinity Brompton, and on one occasion when they were sitting in silence before the service, George lapsed into thinking about the financial difficulties he was undergoing at that moment. Suddenly, out of the blue, Godfrey spoke. 'George, would it help if I sent you a cheque?'

Our time at Crowhurst was the final part of our sabbatical and proved to be formative. We spent several days walking in Ashdown Forest, the home of Christopher Robin and Pooh Bear (Poohsticks Bridge still survives), where wide vistas open up, making it a good place for 'visioning'. We also sat for many hours in the beautiful church of Christ the Healer, where I found my eyes lifted to the window above the high altar. It was very simple: Christ in the centre and 12 arms radiating out from him – a reminder that Christ sends us all out like the Apostles to carry out the mission he lays on us. This vision became overpowering and eventually decisive. We knew what we had to do.

On our return to York we went to see Archbishop Stuart and told him we felt we had to leave the work we loved so much in order to devote ourselves full-time to the ministry of health and healing. If we needed assurance that the Holy

Morris *c.* 1930

Anne's village folk dance
team, late 1920s

Morris in army days,
late 1940s

Anne and Hawkey at 2 St Richard's Walk

Anne at the organ, Chichester Cathedral

Morris as a student,
early 1950s

Morris and Anne with Canon Rupert Brown-Wilkinson and
11-year-old Helen at their wedding in 1955

The Sledmere
Festival,
Yorkshire, 1959

Morris and Anne
in Scarborough,
1960s

Morris and John Yates with Archbishop Donald Coggan,
25 January 1972

Bishop Morris with the Queen Mother

Morris and Anne with Cardinal Basil Hume

Morris and Anne
outside St Mary's Cottage,
Burrswood

Silly hats!

Leaving Burrswood for Whitehill Chase, 1991

The smiley bishop

Morris and Anne's half of the Chantry, Chichester

Morris and Anne lunching at Park House, Bepton, 2005

Morris and John Manchester in Helperthorpe Church, 2007

Morris relaxing with Richard and Virginia Storey
at Settringham, 2007

Spirit was in this, his reply confirmed it. 'Yes, I have also been listening. I have a job for you: you can be Adviser to (Archbishop) Bob and me. That is the good news: now for the bad. There is no money.' We all laughed and I replied, 'If the job needs to be done . . .' and Anne completed the sentence, 'God will provide.' Stuart was impressed that the second part of our reply had come from Anne, the home-maker. From then on we received his support and encouragement, as well as that of the friends with whom we shared the news. It was good that an Archbishop felt the rightness of taking such an initiative, knowing that the experiment would be under the scrutiny of the whole Church. Our loyalty and affection for him made us more determined that it should not fail.

It is always a sad experience to feel that something is coming to an end, especially a fulfilling job in which one has been happy. But we got on with making the necessary arrangements. Frank Baker and his wife Peta invited us to lunch at their home in Groombridge, together with Charles and Anita Longbottom and Raymond Hylton (Lord Hylton). We told them the good news, that I had been invited to be the Healing Adviser to both the Archbishop of Canterbury and York. Then we explained that, though my pension contributions would be continued, there was no money, no home and no expenses! It was obvious to everyone that we needed a support group, and this was best done by forming a charitable trust. What should we call the Trust? Anne made what I believe to be an inspirational suggestion – Acorn. It spoke of growth. She loved her Sussex oak trees, and the acorn was also Dorothy Kerin's emblem, incorporated into the roof of her church of Christ the Healer at Burrswood. Like Julian of Norwich with her hazelnut, Dorothy Kerin had a vision of Christ placing an acorn in her hand and saying to her, 'Tend this with obedience and I will water it with the dew of my love.' So began the Acorn Christian Healing Trust.

During the Christmas period we had the opportunity to think and pray further and look for a good place in which to base ourselves. We should have liked to live in the beautiful cathedral city of Wells, but it would be hard to travel from there. We wondered about Salisbury from where the roads radiate out in fairly straight stretches, so I asked John Bicker-steth if he would countenance one of his assistant bishops living in the neighbouring diocese – purely for the purpose of easing our travelling. To this he readily agreed. As time marched on, however, we still had no house, and decided we would try to get back as much as possible to our cottage in Chichester while carrying out a fairly full diary of travel-ling. In the end we were to spend three and a half months in this peripatetic fashion – once our transport needs had been sorted out: the Church Commissioners, who owned our car, declined a request that I should purchase it from them, but when I happened to mention this in my interview with the Archbishop of Canterbury, he said, 'Leave it to me.' I was later able to buy the car!

Preparations were now being made for farewells in the Diocese of York, and our colleague Leslie Stanbridge, always a great support, arranged services in Norton, Pocklington, Selby Abbey and finally York Minster. I preached at the first three, and the Archbishop at the last. In his sermon, he gave a masterly sketch of Galilee and Jerusalem, contrasting the days of Jesus' carefree ministry of healing, teaching and leisurely journeys, with his experiences, in the place of Judaism's establishment, of controversy and intrigue. Then suddenly he said, 'Morris and Anne are Galilee people: I hope they will have leisurely journeys as they go about their healing and preaching ministry, supported by our love and prayer and blessings.' What an encouragement! Geoffrey

Coffin, the assistant organist – now an organ builder – played us out with glorious music. But it was a very sad occasion for us, having to say goodbye to all our people in and around York, and also to the Minster which had been our cathedral for 25 years. For the first time in our lives, Anne and I felt somewhat on our own, and we both experienced a measure of loneliness as we set our faces to what lay ahead.

Chapter 7

Archbishops' Adviser:
the advent of Acorn

I resigned my See of Selby on 31 March 1983, and we laughed together as we agreed that 1 April was a good day on which to start out on a rather uncertain future. Our total budget was £12,000 plus the generous donations given to us by the Diocese of York and the Archbishops. The £12,000 had come through the kindness of Jack and Jan Head, trustees of the fund which had supported George Bennett's healing ministry. It was a noble tradition in which to follow.

After Easter we drove down to the cottage in Chichester. I had some engagements already in the diary, the first conveniently in Salisbury where we hoped to find a house. Just as we were setting off from the cottage, we received an exciting message from Archbishop Stuart to the effect that he had managed to secure two interest-free loans for us of £20,000 each for this purpose. We thanked God for such a tremendous blessing which seemed to vindicate our whole mission.

One of the loans was from the Church's Central Board of Finance, the other from the Ecclesiastical Insurance Office (EIO) with whom the Church and its clergy were accustomed to arrange insurance. Stuart asked me to make immediate contact with the latter, and when I telephoned, Anne and I were invited to lunch in Gloucester a few days later. In the meantime our host in Salisbury, knowing we were house-hunting, generously invited us to come and stay a while before I was due to lecture and preach at the theological college. At the estate agents, our interest was immediately aroused by a house at 39 St Ann Street. This seemed an appropriate address: the room we were placed in at the theological college was number 39 and the Articles of the Church of England meant it was not a number we were likely to forget! The property was just within our price range, and when we viewed it the following day, we found that it was a typical town house with three floors and a small garden at the back. In our minds' eyes we saw that the first room on the right of the hall might be a study, the next along, which had connecting doors, our dining room. At the end of the hall there was a decent-sized breakfast room and beyond that a small room with a sink that could become a kitchen. Outside the back door there was a cloakroom and a garden. The first floor contained a sizeable drawing room, and two bedrooms with a bathroom in between. Of the two attic rooms on the top floor, one could be our chapel, and the other, looking across the roofs of Salisbury to the back of the White Hart Hotel, might be used for sewing or writing. Knowing that the house would be ideal for us, we made an offer which was eventually accepted.

After carrying out my engagements at Salisbury Theological College, we visited the house once again and realized it would be essential to instal central heating. Our curtains and carpets from Poppleton, which were still fairly new, would fit well, and we were thankful that we and not the diocese had bought them. The owner of the property gave us a date when he would move out, and we made an appointment to see a plumbing firm on site shortly afterwards. We also put down our deposit, and with these preliminaries completed, set out for our luncheon date in Gloucester.

The EIO directors were extremely affable and welcoming. Over a splendid meal in their boardroom we were able to tell them of our hopes for the future, including details of the house in Salisbury and our ideas about the work. I had a fairly full diary for the next three months, which was merciful since we would not be able to move in before then. My official office was to be in the newly opened crypt of St Marylebone parish church: the Rector, Christopher Hamel-Cooke, who had become a great friend, had spent the last year clearing out and converting the crypt, once a burial ground but now disused. With the aid of four noble workmen, he had moved the bodies reverently to the Brookwood cemetery, at which point he asked me to say a Requiem for all the faithful departed. Building work then began on a fine chapel, offices for each of the healing organizations, a doctor's surgery and a restaurant. As Adviser I was to have one of the offices (and the benefit of a part-time secretary) which would be my base and give me a London address.

The directors, our hosts, were most interested in all this – mercifully Christopher insured with them! – and we proceeded to tell them of the two basic thrusts for the work which we inwardly felt laid upon us. The first was to form an 'Apostolate' consisting of pairs of committed Christians, one with medical training, who would act as a sign of Christ the Healer in their area or sphere of work, whether a school, a doctor's surgery, a hospital, a parish or even their own home. During our travels in the first years we would be recruiting priests, doctors, nurses, readers, teachers and other lay people, who would be kept together through a system of prayer and an annual conference, as well as by normal methods of communication. Such became the initial basis of the Acorn Fellowship.

The second thrust was to do some hard work on listening. The name 'Christian Listeners' only came later when

Anne Long joined the staff, but the idea had been formed in my Anne's heart and mind in the organ loft of Chichester Cathedral. There, before the days of closed-circuit television and sound systems, she had to listen intensely to every word and every note, not only to come in at the right time but in the right key. We would develop these themes later on, but for the moment the directors of the EIO were keenly interested and teased out other thoughts through their questions. Before we left, expressing our immense gratitude not only for the lunch but for their generous loan, they asked us to write in the visitors' book. We signed our names, and in the 'address' column wrote, 'Of no fixed abode'. They laughed and said this would be a unique entry: obviously they had entertained no vagrants in their boardroom before now and probably would never do so again.

We needed to return to Yorkshire at this stage, but before doing so led a day on the Christian healing ministry organized by the Stroud churches in Prinknash Abbey, a Roman Catholic community famous in the Anglican Church as a source of supplies of incense. I had a long chat with the Prior, who was as interested in our new work as we were interested in his community, and in the course of the conference we recruited our first doctor for the Apostolate, Paula Lees. Encouraged by our three visits in the south – Salisbury, Gloucester and Prinknash – we drove home to York for the sad business of packing up.

It took us nearly three weeks, but eventually we were ready for the removal firm to collect our furniture, carpets and curtains and store them in Hull until the Salisbury house was ready. On Whit Sunday, we went to York Minster to offer the Sung Eucharist as a thanksgiving. It would be ten years before I conducted a service there again. However, when Anne looked up the daily text in *The Times* the following morning she found that it read, 'You shall go out with singing', and in this spirit we set off on the next stage of our journey.

I was to be commissioned in Wells Cathedral as Adviser to the Archbishops. We made the Swan Hotel our base, attended a rehearsal with my new Bishop, John Bickersteth, and saw to the arrangements for the luncheon after the service which was to take place in the Henderson rooms of the Palace. Several friends had arranged to come, as well as members of our family, and we had a splendid dinner together in the Swan on the night before.

The next morning, its distinctive inverted arches lit up by the sun, the cathedral looked its most glorious and welcoming. The service was beautifully ordered with fine music, and the legal matters were performed by two of the Archbishop of Canterbury's staff, while John Bickersteth, who had asked me to preach, received the oaths. The happy gathering then proceeded to the moated Palace, and we were launched.

One of the first engagements in the diary was a day of teaching in a barn in Stoke D'Abernon owned by Sir Ronald Harris, First Church Estates Commissioner, in which the nearby Yehudi Menuhin School used to give concerts. Sir Ronald kindly invited anyone from the Guildford Diocese to attend, and we managed to recruit as Apostolates James More-Molyneux and his wife Sue, with whom we had dined the night before (he had just read my book and wanted to meet us). At another event in Godalming, we recruited Dr Chris Jagger. Chris, James and Sue would later jointly set up the Loseley Christian Cancer Help Centre.

After this it was time to settle our base in London en route for York where the Archbishops had asked me to return and talk about the job. The Churchwardens of St Marylebone had kindly put me up for membership of the Army and Navy Club in Pall Mall on the corner of St

James' Square, my qualification being that I had held the King's (George VI) commission. Over the years this proved to be a most useful *pied à terre*. Later on I was also invited to become a member of the Royal Society of Medicine because of my job, and this also proved useful, especially for visits to St Marylebone. My publishers, SPCK, were also in Marylebone Road.

In York we usually stayed at the Mount Royale Hotel, which had been the home of one of my aunts when her husband was Medical Officer for the city. You could still make out the name 'Beech House' on the gate post. I was to go to lunch, for once alone, the next day at Bishopthorpe, meeting both Archbishops beforehand. It was John Habgood of York who acted as spokesman. I agreed at once that I should make an annual report of my work. He then told me that there ought to be a body of people to whom I was immediately responsible for the day-to-day working and this should be the Churches' Council for Health and Healing (CCHH), of which I was still chairman. After some questioning of this decision of the Archbishops – and decision it certainly was – I reluctantly agreed, wondering whether it would distance me from their Graces. John Habgood, however, always wrote me gracious and appreciative letters about my annual reports.

The relationship with my colleagues on the CCHH proved to be slightly more difficult. Although I was their chairman, my report had to be submitted to them and they then had to hand it on to the Archbishops with their comments. I dealt with this problem by resigning the chairmanship! It was an odd arrangement for the Anglican Adviser to submit, in the first instance, his report to an ecumenical body. Anne and I were mystified by the whole matter and felt it not to be right. But we persevered with the arrangement.

As we travelled south again we decided that our main task was to engage fully in the work and go for our objectives – the forming of an Apostolate and the training of Christians to listen more intensely to God and to each other. We were soon to add two more goals: first, ministry in the cathedrals of our land, and second, that I should be invited by the bishops to introduce myself in their dioceses, with the aim of encouraging each diocese to appoint its own adviser.

We moved into our new home in Salisbury on St Anne's Day, 26 July 1983. Shortly after, invitations from the bishops began to flow into our London office, and these were to form the basis of the diary for the autumn and into the next year. We paid an early visit to Chichester – not to the cathedral, but to an afternoon session at the Diocesan Synod at Sussex University near Brighton. It was chaired by Bishop Eric Kemp, who had visited us at St Martin-on-the-Hill, and after my talk, he kindly let the question session go on in a most profitable way. There were several doctors present who were members of the synod, as well as interested clergy. Some of the questions I tried to refer to Bishop Eric, especially those concerning diocesan policy, but he asked me to answer them. I hoped I was not treading on any diocesan toes.

One of the next requests was from Ronnie Bowlby, Bishop of Southwark. I was at a slight advantage in that I did know all the bishops, thanks to my membership of the 1978 Lambeth Conference, and I had been present at Ronnie Bowlby's consecration. He kindly asked us to stay with him and to speak at his senior staff meeting. I was used to meetings of eight in York, but there were 17 on the Southwark staff! I felt diffident among so many senior men so early on in the job, but we had a robust discussion afterwards in which Ronnie thought I held my ground. I felt that it had been a good test for me, and Anne and I went home happy and grateful.

Back in the Northern Province, we were invited to stay with David Sheppard, Bishop of Liverpool, and his wife Grace. David and I had been in adjacent colleges at Cambridge, though our paths had never crossed. I had always admired the way he sacrificed an already brilliant career as captain of England and one of the finest opening batsmen, for ordination. A few years before this, at Selby, I had preached at a service of the blessing of oils and renewal of priestly vows in his cathedral. Now he asked me to speak and answer questions at a session with his diocesan healing team. All in all, it was a happy visit, and we were very impressed by the way David and Grace shared together what each had done through the day late at night over cocoa!

Before we left the Northern Province we touched down in Bradford to speak at a day of healing, presided over by the Bishop, Geoffrey Paul, who had been a colleague in the York Diocese as Bishop of Hull. He began his introduction with, 'Many people talk a deal of nonsense about healing, but I've read Morris's book and he talks sense!' I was obliged to him for this commendation, for he had a very good brain. He died far too young when he had hardly been at Bradford three years.

After stopping in London to sort through the mail at the office, and then a few days in our own home in Salisbury, we continued down to Truro, where Bishop Mumford had invited us to stay for a diocesan gathering in the cathedral. While we were sitting waiting as people arrived, he kept making comments like, 'Oh, they've come, have they?', 'Fancy, that's so-and-so', 'Goodness, they've come a long way'. It was quite amusing, but it showed that he knew his flock. We felt that it was an encouraging meeting, and we loved being in Cornwall and among its people again.

At the final Acorn Trustees' meeting of 1983, we laid plans for a big appeal during the following year. Our other two priorities were a conference to bring together those we had recruited as Apostolates, and to implement the vision of listening Anne had been given in the organ loft of Chichester Cathedral. With a second visit to Ireland also being planned and more invitations coming in, 1984 was taking shape.

We launched the appeal at the journalists' church, St Bride's, Fleet Street, and the press turned out in force, with most of the national dailies represented. Frank Baker, our chairman, had asked Charles Longbottom to chair the appeal and this meeting. Dr Peter Nixon, a cardiologist from Weymouth Street, and I spoke, and then the press correspondents asked questions. Afterwards we gave interviews, one of which was on breakfast television the following morning at the TV-am studios. Our publicity officer warned us that the first question would be a Yorker on the middle stump – something like, 'What are you on about when you talk about Christian healing?' There was no place of quiet in the studio building, so we stood in the middle of the entrance hall where pandemonium reigned, and prayed. We were then ushered into the studio to sit on the famous sofa, and a very nice young man from Yorkshire opened the interview with, 'Good morning, Bishop, tell me what you mean by Christian healing'. Obviously I had pondered this and had some answers in my mind. But at the very moment he asked the question, my mind went blank! Then I heard myself say, 'Christian healing is Jesus Christ meeting you at the point of your need.' Such is the wonder of the Holy Spirit. It has become a much-quoted definition.

We had appealed for a quarter of a million pounds, which was quite a sum in those days. The money did not flow in as we had hoped, but Anne and I received a letter after a month or so from the Whitehill Chase Trustees, asking if we would like the use of a country home in Hampshire with six acres and £20,000 a year to run it. We could hardly believe our eyes, and when we telephoned Frank Baker and Charles Longbottom, they could hardly believe their ears! So began a happy and fruitful partnership between the Acorn and Whitehill Trustees, who would provide our headquarters for some time to come. In real terms, our appeal was answered. Once more, God had blessed our act of faith. The next task was to staff the place and advertise for a warden.

We then began to organize the first conference of the Apostolate. So far we had recruited about 20, including two more doctors – one a rheumatologist named Geoffrey Clarke who had cured the arthritis in my fingers with injections and prayer. We only needed a small centre, and chose St Peter's Convent, Woking.

At the same time, we were arranging another gathering of those who might wish to become involved in Anne's vision of listening. Dr Christopher Woodard, a descendant of the Nathaniel Woodard who had founded the Woodard Schools, was very interested and helped us to organize it at his son's large house – fortunately the son didn't seem to object and, in fact, welcomed our intrusion into his life! Christopher Woodard was the author of *A Doctor Heals by Faith: The Reality of Spiritual Healing*, which I recalled being given a copy of as a curate. Not all approved of his methods (though at least he prayed for his patients) and he didn't suffer fools gladly: Anne and I got on famously with him and gave as good as we received. His wife was sweet and long suffering, and indeed under his brusque exterior, Christopher himself possessed a heart of gold.

I invited about a dozen people to the conference, and at the last moment had a letter from a lecturer at St John's College, Nottingham, saying she was on the look-out for a new opportunity and was already a qualified counsellor. I wrote back at once with details of what we had planned and invited her to young Woodard's house – which happened to be in deepest Dorset. Amazingly (this being long before the days of satnav), she arrived. Her name was Anne Long.

Christopher and I opened proceedings with an introductory talk and then invited general discussion. After half an hour, we were all suffering indigestion due to a plethora of ideas, so I suggested a break. One member went next door and played the piano rather well, while others walked or prayed. When we reconvened we were more focused, Anne Long in particular saying some wise things. We agreed on a small working party, consisting of a professional counsellor from Liverpool, Anne Long, Frank Baker and the two of us. When we met in our house in Salisbury a few weeks later, we decided – drawing on the wisdom of the conference – that we would go for listening rather than full-blown counselling; that we should appoint someone who would create a course with modules on the different stages of listening, and that we should name the course Christian Listening. When trained and tested, the successful candidates should be called 'Christian Listeners'. After prayer and lunch, our guests departed for Liverpool and Nottingham. Frank Baker stayed on, and the three of us then agreed that Anne Long was the obvious person to lead this new initiative. Frank said he thought the funds would run to an extra member of staff, but he would consult his fellow trustees. When they responded positively, we wrote to Anne Long, invited her to take on this pioneer job, and rejoiced when she accepted: she became our first member of staff.

Chapter 8

Acorn to sapling

The time of the first Apostolate Conference approached. Most of those we had recruited were able to come, and in the end Anne and I were joined by four doctors, six nurses, five priests, two teachers, and a landowner. It was an exciting conference because they were an expectant group, grateful to be asked to do something for the kingdom and eager to be involved. From the start, our *raison d'être* was that the Apostles had been sent out to proclaim the kingdom (i.e. the fact that God reigns) by healing and preaching. We prayed that each pair of Apostolates might be used to do just that in the service of Christ the Healer, whether in their surgery, hospital, parish, school, parochial church council, or community. Many of the ideas from this conference were used in projects later on; and, as a symbol of our work, Barry Windsor climbed an oak tree in the grounds and took home a pocket full of acorns. At the following year's conference he presented each of us with a tiny oak tree in a pot, a prophetic parable of what would happen to our tiny Acorn.

Of the applicants for another pioneering job, the warden of Whitehill Chase, we decided to interview Roy and Norma Walford, who seemed ideal. Roy was a doctor who had recently been ordained, while Norma was a nurse; they had both been missionaries in Pakistan and had a family.

The Trustees, Anne and I offered them the post and they moved into Whitehill Chase in 1985. At first, with only a skeleton staff, life was not easy for them, but they contributed at staff and Trustees' meetings, and inaugurated the healing Eucharist which has taken place on Tuesdays ever since. Gradually a team of local supporters was built up, and we began to think of holding conferences on a small scale, having only the main house for accommodation.

The previous year, we had been invited to return to Ireland. Jim Farrar had taken over from Stanley Baird as Warden of Healing and kindly made all the arrangements for what was going to be a longer visit, including the north as well as the south. Setting off in the car from Salisbury, we decided to spend the night in Holyhead on Holy Island, and the vicar there agreed to put us up provided I would preach at a healing service that evening. The church was full of clergy and people from all over Anglesey, and having finished my sermon and begun on the prayers, I was somewhat startled by a loud noise outside the church reminiscent of Concorde landing. In came a leather-coated figure removing a crash helmet – one has a good view from the pulpit! – who sat down at the back, divested himself of his variety of cameras (he was of course the press photographer), then looked around, apparently wondering what all these people were doing on their knees. Gradually, however, he knelt down himself and seemed lost in prayer. Along with everyone else, he came up for the laying on of hands. We heard later that one of the vicar's colleagues had bumped into the photographer shortly afterwards and asked, 'What happened to you last week? I thought you had only come for a quick happy snap.' He was slow to reply, but spoke most sincerely: 'It was those people. Those people praying. It got me – really powerfully. I felt I had to join them and so I knelt too. It's changed my life. I really have turned to Christ.' I've often told this story to encourage congregations that one never knows what may happen when they are at prayer. The Holy Spirit blows where he wills.

The following morning, after a calm and pleasant crossing, Jim Farrar met us at Dun Laoghaire, and we started on the long road north to Armagh. We felt privileged to be staying with Archbishop John Armstrong and his wife, who had shown bravery and humble fair-mindedness in the midst of the Troubles and had received death threats as a result. The very evening of our healing service, in the numinous and historic cathedral of the Archdiocese of Armagh, a warning was issued that the Army and RUC were looking for a bomb in the city. They had already searched the Roman Catholic Cathedral.

The next day was Sunday and the Archbishop drove us to one of the churches in the city for the early service. I noticed that every garage we passed was boarded up, and when I remarked on this, we were told they had all been blown up for refusing to pay the IRA protection money. Later, walking to the church a short distance away where I was due to preach, Anne and I were a little alarmed to find ourselves in the middle of a British Army patrol (still looking for the bomb!). Anne wasn't at all happy to discover that I would be preaching from an open pulpit, because it was not long after the pastors at a Pentecostal church had been gunned down. In our hearts we prayed for the protection of the holy angels for everyone, and mercifully the service passed without incident.

That afternoon, we had arranged to visit the centre of reconciliation at beautiful Rostrevor, where 'the mountains of Mourne come down to the sea'. We were very impressed with the work going on there and warmed to the warden and all he had achieved.

I had been invited to preach at the annual Synod service

for the Church of Ireland – a rare privilege for an Englishman – and some days later, as we were robing before the service in St Patrick's Cathedral, Dublin, John Armstrong came up and said, 'Thank God you had to go on to Rostrevor last Sunday. That very night the bomb they had been looking for exploded. The next morning we found your bed completely covered and torn by shards of glass.'

Our visits to Ireland had certainly widened our experience and given us a larger view. We realized what an immense task there would be in terms of healing and reconciliation once the Troubles were over. Meanwhile we felt an obligation to pray for the country, a portion of which was part of our own.

On our return to England, Anne Long suggested that she should live in Stanstead Abbotts to be near her friend Margaret Jones, vice-principal of All Nations Christian College. This seemed to be an excellent idea, for our friends Cocky and Joan Trower lived nearby in Stansteadbury and would happily put us up when we wanted to meet with Anne and Margaret. At that time they were planning three pilot courses in Christian Listener training – at the village church in Stanstead Abbotts, at a commuter church in Billericay, Essex, and at a town centre church in Reading.

The year 1985 saw the gradual consolidation of the Acorn family. We now had the Acorn Apostolate, the Christian Listeners, headquarters at Whitehill Chase, and our own ministry under the Archbishops, which saw us travelling the country to preach, teach and minister. Requests from the bishops continued to come in. Robert Runcie kindly invited me to speak at the Canterbury Synod, where the meeting was chaired by a sensitive senior priest. At his elbow sat the diocesan lawyer who offered constant advice, but mercifully the chairman, to misquote Alexander Pope, 'Sometimes advice took and sometimes not'. When I had finished my talk and questions were slow in coming, the lawyer almost immediately whispered, 'You can close this down now.' Mercifully the chairman stood his ground, and eventually we had a very full and constructive debate. I felt I had indeed been saved by grace and not by the law!

We held the 1985 Apostolate Conference at the Theological College in Salisbury. Roy and Eira Lawrence came for the first time to this conference, as did Peg Price from Portsmouth and Roy and Norma Walford from Whitehill Chase. In one year we had more than doubled our members, and there was real enthusiasm for the work. We all left in good heart, and I took the initiative of beginning my third book, *Journey to Wholeness*, which was to be published the next year. (My second, a Lent course entitled *The Christian Adventure*, had come out in 1983.) I used the teaching of biblical journeys and wrote in the foreword:

> The vision of our work and witness is that all will travel together as the healed and healing community. The purpose of the journey is a healed creation, not just a collection of new individuals. The whole is greater than the sum of its parts and that is why under God, it is a journey to wholeness. The healing of the churches and of the caring professions is therefore of prime necessity, as well as the healing of society and nations. There is much business to be done on the journey. Pray we may listen more intently to our marching orders.

Anne and I began to visit the theological colleges and were glad to see Paul Bradshaw, an ordinand from our Scarborough parish and now an expert in liturgy, in action on the staff at Cuddesdon, Oxford. On another visit to Cranmer Hall, Durham, we were able to call on Michael and Joan Ramsey in their retirement, and also on Phyllis, widow of Alan Richardson who had been Dean of York at the time of my consecration. Visits to other theological colleges were to take place over the years, including Wycliffe Hall, Oxford, and Oak Hill in London, and while we lived in Salisbury I gave an annual lecture at the theological college there. We felt that seeds were sown on each of these visits, and later on it was good to know that *The Christian Healing Ministry* had become the standard work on the subject for theological students.

By 1986 we needed a larger centre for our annual conference, and settled on Cardinal Basil Hume's pastoral centre at London Colney. It had originally been built as a rather magnificent Anglican convent and had a beautiful chapel and good accommodation. This proved to be a formative conference, with the Apostolate pairs responding creatively to the challenge to advance the work. James More-Molyneux and Chris Jagger, with the support of their wives and helped by their chaplain, began a Christian Cancer Help Centre at Loseley Park near Guildford. They insisted on putting 'Christian' first because after visiting other centres, including the famous one in Bristol, they knew this to be the essential element. Meetings were held once and later twice a month, with invitations going out to those suffering from cancer and their relatives or friends to come for the day. Lunch, worship, prayer with the laying on of hands, meditation and a discussion comprised the programme, and over the years these days have proved greatly beneficial, with many 'remissions'. A third Tuesday in the month is now set aside for sufferers from Parkinson's disease. James and Sue More-Molyneux have built a fine chapel, and a meeting room which is named after Thomas More, one of James' ancestors. The work continues, with many blessings.

Other initiatives began to come on stream. In Stafford, Sheila Young began the John Young Foundation in memory of her doctor husband, who had died just as he was beginning to be a leader in the healing ministry. The Foundation still actively promotes Christian healing and wholeness. In Maidstone, Margaret Doak opened what would become the Shalom Centre, and in 2006 she was awarded the Cross of St Augustine by the Archbishop of Canterbury for her contribution to the counselling and healing ministry. In Milton Keynes, Dr Linda Davis, who suffers from MS, and her husband John began a project called Harmony House, which has developed into the Harmony House Christian Healing Centre; and in Bradford Cathedral, John Richardson, the Dean, who was by this time an Acorn Trustee, began a healing initiative. Today the cathedral's Healing Prayer Group has 16 members and incorporates Listeners, a number of health professionals of various disciplines, and some Lay Assistants, who take Holy Communion to the housebound and those in care.

In the meantime, Anne Long was making great strides with her Christian Listener (CL) work, helped part time by Margaret Jones when her college duties permitted. Dr Moy Gill, who had a practice in Ware, also offered to become a staff member, and on a tour of the north, Anne made contact with Sharon Stinson, an American and one of David Watson's elders at St Michael le Belfrey. Sharon was greatly enamoured of the whole concept of CL, and very soon offered herself as a full-time member of the Acorn staff. She and Moy Gill came down to Burrswood to be commissioned in the Church of Christ the Healer, giving CL a presence in both north and south. Like us with the Apostolate, Anne had a travelling and directing role.

In 1986, Anne, Moy and Margaret (who had now retired and was working for CL in the north-west) drew on their experience in the pioneer projects in Stanstead Abbotts, Billericay and Reading to write a CL manual. An Apostolate manual was also produced by the staff – Apostolates and CLs – over an enjoyable if hardworking 24 hours at the White Hart Hotel in Salisbury, where we took over the St Ann's suite. It was good to have occasions like these when we could meet together: my Anne and I had found that pioneering work could be a lonely road, and though we tried to maintain prayerful telephone fellowship, it was obvious that each of us involved was carrying a heavy load. At Whitehill Chase, Roy and Norma in particular were struggling. Things had not worked out as we had hoped, and sadly at this point, we had to bid them a grateful and fond farewell.

After this we had a change of chairmanship of the Trustees: Frank Baker, who had led us so well through the first five years, was replaced by Charles Longbottom who remained in the post for the remainder of our time in Acorn. A good fundraiser, he was to see us through some difficult times financially; he was also the architect of a new, very close partnership with the Whitehill Chase Trustees, whose chairman, the Revd John Russell, became one of our Trustees.

It so happened that David and Dorothy Smethurst were staying at Whitehill Chase. David had been Dean of Hong Kong for a short time and was now home, looking for another job. We all thought that he and Dorothy, who had been a headteacher, had the right gifts and ideas, and eventually they were appointed as wardens. From this point on, Anne and I felt that we should hold more regular meetings so as to build staff cohesion: our finances had been so parlous when Acorn was first set up that these had been cut down on the grounds of cost.

On the home front, we were developing a ministry to cathedrals. With her 13 years' experience at Chichester, Anne had always had a hunch that the mother church of a diocese was one place where the message should be heard.

At a service in our own cathedral of Wells, organized by the healing committee of the diocese, the Bishop, John Bickersteth, officiated while I preached. At the laying on of hands, we both stood at the centre of the altar rail, and among the many who came up was a man whose legs seemed to be crippled. It was John's turn to say the prayer, after which the man walked away normally. Later on, we learned he had been to healing services in his parish for years, but today had received healing. I always felt it was not only for his sake but for John's and mine. It certainly spoke to John: at the end of the service in the sanctuary he said, 'Morris, take my crozier and give the blessing.' I said, 'But John, you are the Diocesan Bishop and this is your cathedral.' 'Do as I say!' I replied very diffidently, 'I do it under obedience to you.' I felt it to be a wonderful gesture, perhaps a thanksgiving for what he had received at the service, and was humbled.

Acorn was continuing to grow, and it seemed to Anne and me that it would help if we could not only 'sing from the same hymn book', but also pray from the same prayer book. Anne had generously sacrificed her sewing space to give me an inspirational writing room at the top of the house, and here I began compiling my new book, *The Healing House of Prayer*. The idea came from Leslie Weatherhead's fine *A Private House of Prayer*, and was suggested by my editor at Hodder and Stoughton, Edward England. In the introduction I acknowledged my debt not only to him but to Leslie Weatherhead.

Born out of the Methodist tradition, *A Private House of Prayer* has helped Christians of all denominations to draw nearer to their Lord. Here I am able to speak from experience, for its creative spirituality, which meets all occasions, has greatly helped Anne and me,

particularly during the 'wilderness' periods of our lives.
It has helped to transform those periods into times of
preparation and renewal for the next step on the journey.

I offered a theme for each day of the month, and there were
seven 'rooms' in the daily house. The book was published in
1987 and has been widely used, even in prisons.

That year saw us on the move once more. After the last
Apostolate conference, we had been trying to envisage a
way in which we could have groups of the Apostolate together for prayer, fellowship and training. Our first thought
was the Crowhurst Christian Healing Centre, where I was
chairman of the Divine Healing Mission. We hoped we
might build a house there and make use of the centre's
conference facilities. But there were difficulties. Then
Gareth Tuckwell, director of Burrswood, invited us for
lunch, and over the meal and a leisurely time afterwards we
told him of our search for a place in which to live and train
the Apostolate. His response came as a wonderful surprise,
a gift from God. He asked if we would like to come and live
at Burrswood: St Mary's cottage was shortly to become
vacant and would suit Anne and me, while Chapel House
(the guest house) would accommodate those who came on
the courses. It seemed the perfect answer, and we accepted
gratefully.

Meanwhile the work of travelling continued. Three good
days in the Choir Festival cathedrals of Hereford, Gloucester and Worcester were followed by our first visit to St
Albans Abbey at the invitation of the Dean, Peter Moore.
After I had given my talk, he said to the assembled company, 'Now, who wants to attack the bishop?' I'm happy to
say no one drew their sword! We actually had a very constructive discussion. In the morning he kindly showed us

round the Abbey, and it was nice to be back where we had often repaired for Evensong in our Uxbridge days.

More conferences were being arranged by the local churches. On arrival at All Saints, Northampton, I was handed a note from the bishop which said that he did not want me to use the laying on of hands publicly in the church, because in his view such ministry was reserved for the sick room only. I remember we all sat round the vestry table – there were at least 20 clergy – and quietly prayed for guidance. One of the young curates broke the silence: 'Why don't we give each other the Peace? At least our hands will touch each other.' And so we did. The Peace was particularly meaningful that evening.

The following weekend we were in Cambridge staying with Lady Nan Willink, mother of my old college friend, Charles, who had organized a strenuous two days for us. On the Saturday, which happened to be my birthday, I was to give a lecture at a healing day at St James's church. I was somewhat alarmed on arrival to find the Regius Professor of Divinity, Charlie Moule, and the distinguished church lawyer, Prebendary Garth Moore, sitting in the front row. They turned down my offer to change places! I would gladly have sat at their feet. Afterwards we were able to spend time in Heffers bookshop and at my old college of Trinity.

On the Sunday, Nan had arranged for us to go to St Edward, King and Martyr, off King's Parade, where she and her husband Harry used to worship when he was Master of Magdalene. I was to preach and celebrate a late Eucharist, and we were excited to see Charles Claxton in the congregation, who as Bishop of Blackburn had presented me at my consecration. In the evening, after preaching in Chapel at Trinity Hall, we were entertained by the Master, Morris Sugden. He was a chemist and on many ecological committees including one on fuels, so he knew all about the Selby coalmine. It was around this time that Anne began to talk about global warming, which I did not understand at all, as there was no public discussion about it in those far-off days. But Anne knew it was coming, and this was not the only occurrence of her being ahead of her time. In hindsight I wondered if it had ever been discussed at one of Morris Sugden's ecological committees.

While we were in Cambridge, Anne Long was in Oxford. She had begun a series of visits to theological colleges, asking the principal in each case to invite students from the local medical school for joint seminars with the college students on Christian Listening. Anne would be the tutor. She saw this as another way in which CL, like the Apostolate, could bridge the gap between the Church and medicine. The fact that two groups of students would meet was good in itself; that they should meet to experience Christian Listening together would be a decisive move forward. St Stephen's House pioneered the scheme and it was followed up in Oak Hill College, London, and Queen's College, Birmingham, the whole operation being wholeheartedly agreed as a part of Acorn's strategy.

*　　*　　*

In the late summer of 1987 we began the sad job of packing up our home once again. We had spent a very happy four years in Salisbury, but it was obvious that Burrswood beckoned. Not only did it offer us opportunities of training the Apostolate, we also looked forward to living in a place we had come to love on our frequent visits and to being neighbours of Gareth and Mary Tuckwell.

We reached Burrswood late one evening in early October, and were welcomed by two of Dorothy Kerin's colleagues (Dorothy herself died in 1963), Gladys Modine and her friend Kathleen Nest, who had kindly stayed up to greet us. When our furniture arrived the next morning, we once more began the process of setting up house. St Mary's cottage was a fifteenth-century timbered building, and Acorn had generously made many improvements, completely renovating the bathroom and putting in a new French window in what was to be my study. The cottage was situated at the top of the drive close to St Luke's, where Gareth and Mary lived, and adjacent to the old apple store which now housed the office complex. Just beyond, the drive continued past Chapel House to the main buildings and the church of Christ the Healer. There were other cottages dotted round the hill which were occupied by community members. Three of Dorothy Kerin's other colleagues, Princess Marina Chavchavadze, 'Boccy' Cauldwell and Johanna Ernst, lived in the old stable block near the offices. Peter and Paddy Hunt, the hardworking gardeners who had 50 acres to care for, lived in a house towards the farm which lay beyond the main buildings, as did the chaplain David Flagg. Jill Lightfoot (the sacristan) and Sophia Burchnell (in charge of Chapel House) lived up the hill.

The great storm of October 1987, which occurred exactly two weeks later, was a traumatic affair for the south of the country. It was at its wildest around 4 a.m., mercifully too early to catch those going to work, for the roads – from Devon to Kent – were littered with fallen trees. I shall never forget the moment the storm hit Burrswood, its eerie whine so loud that we did not hear one tree falling at the back door of our cottage and another at the front. It took the community 24 hours to saw a way out to the main road. Gareth was first on the scene, and I remember his words: 'That has opened up a few new vistas', a prophetic remark for all of us who were seeking new visions of what God wanted us to do. The buildings were covered with a mix of sand and salt water, probably from the Bay of Biscay, which took ages to remove from the windows. All the power lines were down and it was three weeks before we were reconnected, the electricity boards having to bring in engineers from various parts of Britain. We managed for a week by candlelight, but eventually the place had to be closed down for a fortnight, and we found ourselves on the road again, going off to stay with friends.

On our return we began to plan our training sessions for the Apostolate. We thought that ten members should be the maximum number at a time, preferably less, and in fact we usually averaged eight. As Burrswood had a constant flow of visitors, we would book Chapel House well in advance, and also the drawing room in the main building as the training room. The course would last two and a half to three days, either over a weekend, or from tea on Tuesday to lunch on Friday. We would have two sessions in the morning, one after tea, a discussion after supper, and fit in with the worship in the church of Christ the Healer. Afternoons were free. The sessions would be on Bible study, visioning and the practical working out on the ground of situations in which those attending were involved. Beginning in the late autumn and continuing about every two months or so for the next four years, the Apostolate courses helped establish a deep fellowship among us all. The doctors and nurses especially welcomed the chance to see something of the working together of the Church and medicine in Burrswood.

The Christian Listener project was also progressing well. In 1987, 59 people had been trained at five courses, while the following year 45 people were trained at four – not only to be Listeners themselves, but also to train others. In fact, CL work was now going on in 14 dioceses. There were four groups in York, Winchester and Rochester, three groups in Bath and Wells, Chelmsford, Oxford and St Albans, two in

Chichester and Peterborough, and one in Canterbury, London, Lichfield, Birmingham and Southwark. CL members began to work in drop-in centres, in hospitals – which helped the nursing staff to listen to patients – in bereavement groups, in Life groups, in church pastoral care groups, in contact with GPs' surgeries and in the occasional psychiatric hospital. Later on, CL workers were to be found in schools, prisons and factories. The work was endless, for sadly in today's world people have little time to listen to others.

Between the Apostolate courses there was much work to be done. Bath and Wells had appointed the first diocesan adviser on healing, and Anne and I began to arrange conferences for other potential advisers. First I wrote to the bishops of dioceses across the middle of England; then Nigel Beazley, whom we had just appointed as administrator of Acorn, advised me to write to the Roman Catholic bishops as well. (Nigel was RC.) This I did, inviting them to send to the conference at Launde Abbey their 'representative' or 'observer' (mostly the Roman Catholics specified this category) or, if they had already appointed one, their 'adviser'. It was an exciting conference, and many good priests were subsequently appointed as advisers by their bishops. Anne and I were especially grateful to our friend Paul Burbridge, by now Dean of Norwich, who showed great vision and leadership during the sessions.

Next we asked the bishops of the north, both Anglican and Roman Catholic, if they would send a representative/ observer to a conference at Ampleforth Abbey. This was to be the most exciting and productive of all the conferences: no fewer than six out of the seven Roman Catholic dioceses were represented, and 12 out of the 13 Anglican. Nigel Beazley came with us, and on the way we stopped off at Leicester where Canon Dr Russell Hunt and Mrs Freda

Aldridge, our Apostolate pair, presided over several initiatives. Freda had been left some land by her father and she had begun to build old people's homes which were staffed by Christians. Freda had a gift of encouraging the residents to be occupied in some worthwhile project or other, and when we went into the day room in one home, we were impressed by the zeal of the 75- to 95-plus-year-olds enthusiastically 'knitting for Bangladesh'. It was an uplifting environment in which to live.

Ampleforth has a fine setting overlooking the plain of York, and it was a joy to worship with the monks in their abbey while staying in an excellently equipped retreat home. I invited a few outside speakers, including the Bishop of Blackburn, Alan Chesters, who had been crucifer at my father's funeral in 1953, and Monsignor Michael Buckley, who assisted me with the worship. It was agreed by the conference that I should write to the bishops who had sent people, asking that they appoint their nominated representative as their adviser on the ministry of health and healing. This resulted in a steady stream of appointments, and looking after them became a mammoth task. Nigel Beazley would come over to Burrswood once a month to assist me, but eventually we appointed Canon Roy Lawrence to care for the advisers and bring them together regularly. Roy was the adviser for Chester and a part-time member of the Acorn staff. Like us, he had sat at George Bennett's feet, and he would go on to write several books on the Christian healing ministry, including *How to Pray When Life Hurts* and *The Practice of Christian Healing*.

The third conference, for the south, was also well attended by Anglican and Roman Catholic representatives. In hindsight, it was probably a mistake to have the first half of the week at Burrswood and the second at Whitehill Chase, because the participants (not to say the leaders) became rather tired by the end. Nevertheless, most of the bishops appointed their representatives as their diocesan advisers, with the result that the whole of England was now covered. Every diocese had contributed to the formation of this valuable body of people involved with us in the service of the Christ who heals. It was one of the most constructive pieces of work in our time at Acorn as Archbishops' Adviser.

I must not give the impression that Anne and I had forgotten that leisure is a necessary part of a healthy life! We loved exploring East Sussex which neither of us knew very well. Walks on Beachy Head were a pleasure, and of course visits to various hostelries for a good lunch, a pastime Anne enjoyed for the rest of her life. Our favourites were the Netherfield, a fine Lutyens-like house north of Battle, which is now a private dwelling, Beauport Park, on the other side of Battle, and one or two of the hotels on the front at Eastbourne, particularly the Lansdowne. Nearer home we often went to the Spa Hotel in Tunbridge Wells. We also tried to have a daily walk in the grounds of Burrswood, often visiting the heron on the lake at the bottom of the drive, and enjoying the gardens, which with their acers, maples, beeches and chestnuts, were particularly beautiful in the autumn.

There was now another small book to write, *Twenty Questions About Healing*, which brought together the questions I was most frequently asked at conferences and lectures, and offered my answers. It was published by SPCK in 1988, and appeared to fill a gap as a starters' guide.

Chapter 9

The enlarging ministry

Many people came to stay at Burrswood, and we received a constant trickle of visitors. Among the first was one of Anne's old choristers, who had diligently followed up our changes of address. I recall his appearance at the door and his diffident question, 'I don't expect the name Peter Begbie means anything to you?' 'Of course it does,' I replied. 'Anne has often spoken about you. Come in!' Peter had been a chorister at the cathedral at the same time as David Graebe, the organ architect, and Anne really enjoyed catching up with him – and with David too, when we discovered he lived not far away. His beautiful house, Chant Stream Cottage, has a fine garden with over 50 species of rhododendron, and guests are transported around it on a model railway David built himself! He owns about two dozen clocks whose chimes he somehow manages to synchronize. It's quite a sound.

Another musician Anne was delighted to see again was John Rose, now the director of music at Hartford College, Connecticut, whom we had first met when he came to give a recital at St Martin's in Scarborough. John was a third-generation 'descendant' of Widor through Marcel Dupré and Virgil Fox, and on one visit Anne presented him with a copy of Widor's composition, *Lauda Sion*.

Some time later, John was due to give a celebrity recital at St Paul's Cathedral, and Anne and I found ourselves sitting under the dome at about the place we had been for my ordination 33 years previously. We noticed that *Lauda Sion* was on the programme, and before John played it he came down from the organ loft to address the audience. 'Two years ago,' he began, 'I was given this piece of music by a pupil of a pupil of Widor, partly because I am also a pupil one generation further down. The person who gave it to me was Anne Maddocks, who before her marriage was assistant organist in Chichester Cathedral, where she gave the first performance of the Poulenc Organ Concerto in your country. I am happy to say she is here tonight with her husband, and I dedicate this performance to her in gratitude.' Anne was greatly moved by this and by his performance of the piece, which has always been one of her favourite compositions. The following day she had a happy and memorable birthday, when John joined us for a celebration lunch.

Down south at Loseley Park, where James More-Molyneux and Dr Chris Jagger were making great progress with their Christian cancer help centre, about 30 of us assembled one glorious summer's day for a time of reflection in the chapel, followed by a joyful lunch in the barn. Cameras were much in evidence. Another outing from which we derived spiritual blessing and direction was a visit to St Wite's (pronounced Witta) Well at Whitchurch Canonicorum, near Bridport in Dorset, organized by the vicar of the parish church, John Affleck. After a short service at the holy well, followed by a picnic lunch, we filed into the parish church, which has its own ancient shrine of healing, and there, in the repository at the shrine, placed our prayer requests as pilgrims had done over the centuries.

★   ★   ★

In 1988, Anne and I made a major tour of the three north-ernmost dioceses – Durham, Newcastle and Carlisle. In Durham, Michael Perry (the Archdeacon) and his wife kindly had us to stay at their home in the cathedral close. After worship on the Sunday morning and visits to the shrine of St Cuthbert and the fine Galilee chapel, we went off to Sunderland where I preached at a service of healing. That night, though it was May, a cold spell began, and we couldn't get warm in bed even with our overcoats on! Poor Anne caught a chill and was unable to accompany me the next day. While Mrs Perry looked after her in front of a coal fire, Michael took me to a gathering of clergy he had assembled in one of the university lecture rooms. David Jenkins, who had been our theologian at the 1981 'Health for the Eighties' conference, was by this time Bishop of Durham and came to preside over what turned out to be a very positive morning with some useful questions. In a lighter moment, someone asked why I had qualified an item with the word 'particularly' instead of 'especially'. Amid much laughter by us all, David said in a loud aside, 'Yes, I had noticed that.' He was very solicitous over Anne's health and sent her his love and best wishes for resuming our tour. In fact she was back with me the fol-lowing day, when Michael took us to call on John and Mary Moorman in their retirement. We found them both in excellent form and reminisced about our times at Chichester, as well as our mutual visits when John was Bishop of Ripon. He also related many stories from Vati-can II where he had been the chief Anglican observer – they were both great admirers of Pope John XXIII – while Mary told us she had just completed another work on Wordsworth. How good it was to see them again, espe-cially as it turned out this was to be the last time. When he died, John graciously left me his pectoral cross of five amethysts because I was his first student to become a bishop.

While we were in the Durham Diocese, Anne and Brian Black, and Peter and Sue Ward had us to stay at the large house in Gateshead they had bought for themselves and their families in order to be a sign of the healing Christ. We were advised to bring our car in behind their (locked) gates otherwise 'it may not be there in the morning', which told us something about the area in which they had chosen to live. The house was a visiting centre for clergy, doctors, parish groups, local people and groups from the diocese. The Apostolates held seminars, teaching courses and times of fellowship in which they would talk of the Acorn vision and give training in our methods of working together. They were being much used, and we greatly admired the initiative they had taken and the sacrifices they were making. Later on, Anne and Peter were to become members of the Acorn staff, having moved to Cumbria to set up a new centre and work closely with the Bishop of Carlisle.

After this we crossed the Tyne and entered Newcastle. There I gave a seminar to the medical staff and clergy who had assembled in one of the city hospitals, and spent a day in the cathedral, where a heavily attended session was sensitively chaired by the Provost. In Carlisle Cathedral, a day or two later, I preached at Evensong when the theme was the Christian healing ministry. Anne was delighted to find that Jeremy Suter, who had been one of her successors at Chichester, was the cathedral organist. He had found two beautiful anthems on the theme of healing for the service.

Afterwards we discovered that John Richardson (the Dean of Bradford and an Acorn Trustee) had been in the congregation. We drove down the M6 in convoy and, before continuing on home, John updated us on his Apostolate initiative in the cathedral over dinner at Graythwaite Manor in

Grange-over-Sands. Anne and I were glad to be able to relax in our old bolt-hole for a few days amid the beauty of the Lakes.

*   *   *

During the year another book had been turning over in my mind. Living at Burrswood, we had absorbed much of the atmosphere of Dorothy Kerin and her vision. We also had the advantage of frequent talks with her colleagues, who were now senior members of the Community and full of wisdom and experience. From Marina and Bocky, Gladys and Kathleen, Johanna Ernst and Maria (who had both been head nurses during Dorothy's time), Kathleen Davis and Marisa (who lived in the village) we learned a great deal, and Anne was good at recalling things which had particularly struck her in these conversations. In fact, she contributed much to the production of the book, for while I wrote in the evenings, Anne would play the piano, and her music so inspired me that eventually I found it harder to write if she was not playing. In *The Vision of Dorothy Kerin* I tried to demonstrate Dorothy's unflagging faith which inspired her every move – her prayer life was deeply impressive – and to show how her compassion and understanding touched everyone she met. Her spirit lives on in the expanding work of Burrswood today as well as in the international work of the Acorn foundation.

In the Acknowledgements, I expressed my debt to Anne:

Last but not least, those who know me know that it really is 'us' and that none of the work or writing would be possible without my wife, Anne. She survived eight gruelling weeks of constant writing and plied me with good meals and Mozart, prayer and laughter, love

and Elgar, so that the work came to completion. I
thank her from my heart.

I then added:

> Together we dedicate this book to the Christian heal-
> ing communities and organizations, for whom the
> acorn is a treasured symbol of growth, and the coming
> of God's Kingdom.

Donald Coggan kindly wrote the Preface to the first edition,
published by Hodder and Stoughton in 1991, and Gareth
Tuckwell to the second which came out in 1999.

At this point, since the work was growing so speedily, our
Trustees voted to fund an increase in staff. One of those to
come on board was Trevor Nash, who had been chaplain to
St George's Hospital, Hyde Park Corner (now the Lanes-
borough Hotel) before becoming Archdeacon of Winchester. He organized a splendid day for us in Winchester town
hall under the chairmanship of Colin James the Bishop, at
which Dr Gordon Taylor of the BMA (one of our Trustees)
and I spoke. There was an enthusiastic response which
Trevor ably harnessed and organized, and when I suggested
we ask him to join Acorn, everyone happily agreed. At the
same time, Anne Long proposed one of her former students
at St John's College, Nottingham, Russ Parker. Russ was
Vicar of Coalville in the Leicester Diocese and came with
ecumenical experience: he had been born a Roman Catholic in Birkenhead, where he later served as a Baptist minister, before being ordained into the Anglican Church. He
has always delighted in reminding us that Anne and I interviewed him in the ladies' drawing room of the Army and
Navy Club! (We were staying there for London meetings,
and as Anne was present, could gain entry to what was

actually the most comfortable room in the place.) Russ was eventually to succeed us as director of Acorn.

As the number of people working under Acorn's umbrella had increased so dramatically, our work was cut out to keep all the contacts going. Every outside visit by staff members, every training/visionary course we held at Burrswood, and every conference at Whitehill Chase increased this flow, while the work of the diocesan advisers and the healing houses ensured that the healing dimension of the gospel was being given space in the proclamation of the kingdom and the life of the Church.

*   *   *

It was during our time at Burrswood that Archbishop Michael Ramsey died. Before their final move to Oxford, we had arranged to visit him and Joan at their flat in the medieval part of Bishopthorpe in York. When we reached the gatehouse we were amazed to see huge notices saying 'No cars beyond this point', 'Turn left and park in the garages area'. We had always driven up to the house before, but thought we had better obey. When we rang their bell, Michael came to the door and asked urgently, 'Where's your car?' We explained about the notices and he said, 'Oh, you shouldn't have taken any notice!' The dear man was quite upset. Joan and Anne settled down for a long chat, including in their conversation a duck who made frequent appearances on the windowsill looking for food, while I asked Michael several questions about his life and archi-episcopate. What, I wondered, was he most thankful for in his ministry? He mentioned three things: that he had given unity priority, that he had not lost his head during the *Honest to God* debate, and that he had 'preferred to devote some time to people even to the neglect of some administration' (much laughter). I then asked him about the Church today. He said there were too many reports and too few good books; that bishops were given overmuch to administration; and that the price of disunity was too great a price to pay for women priests. In general discussion he made various points: he felt that Basil Hume was a great spiritual leader who had taken the Church into the community instead of just keeping the show going. Of other religions, he believed we should always admit something of God in them, but that we must proclaim with ever deeper conviction and commitment the uniqueness and power and glory of Christ. He also felt that in today's world the greatest disaster is a despiritualized, irreligious human consciousness. As Anne and I knelt for his blessing for the last time, he prayed that we and all Christ's Church would be given grace to serve God and his people.

With a sense of uncertainty as to the future, we took an affectionate leave, but Michael insisted on walking down to the garages with us to see us into our car.

Another delightful visit was to Donald and Jean Coggan at Sissinghurst. Their home, Kingshead House, had once been a hostelry, and as we entered, Donald began to explain its history and geography, ending with the information that there was a cellar. 'So,' Anne commented, 'it's a dry house.' Whereupon, quick as a flash, Donald replied, 'Well, it is now!' Jean told us how she had been in touch with Anne Long, and that several in the parish had been on a Christian Listener course. A CL group was in the process of being formed.

In the afternoon we set out for Leeds Castle, Donald insisting on sitting in the back with Jean. On our approach we were confronted by a notice which read, 'No cars beyond this point'. 'Drive straight on,' commanded Donald from the rear. Soon we were stopped by a security man, but when

Donald waved a bit of paper at him, he immediately let us through. The same thing happened again a little later, and eventually we came to the drawbridge. 'Positively NO vehicles beyond this point', we read. I was wondering what to do when the usual command issued forth: 'Drive straight on!' Nervously I proceeded into the castle, where we found a place in which to park and had a good laugh over our progress. Apparently, because of his position, Donald had been given written permission to enter the castle at any time.

The Coggans showed us round all the apartments, including the bedroom they used to stay in and the beautiful chapel Donald had rededicated on their last visit. We felt that we were walking in history: the medieval castle has hosted many important events over the centuries, including the 1978 Arab–Israeli peace talks, and is still used for high-level political conferences today. After our tour, we sat out on the terrace overlooking the moat in the summer sunshine, and admired the glorious view.

Around this time, we had a particularly enjoyable visit to London. Canon Edwyn Young, after a significant ministry as a theatre chaplain in Liverpool (he had ministered to my cousin Helen when she appeared in a show in New Brighton in Wirral), had become chaplain at the Queen's Chapel of the Savoy. On arrival, he found that the walls of the large vestry were rather bare and asked the churchwardens if he could put up some of his pictures. They readily agreed, probably expecting a Canaletto and a few Constables, so imagine their surprise when the following Sunday they found the walls covered with photographs of stage stars, sparsely clad dancers, and chorus girls, the prints being inscribed with messages such as 'To darling Edwyn, all my love, ——'! As a vestry wall, it must have been unique in the Church of England! Later, Edwyn distinguished himself by becoming the first 'archdeacon' of the hotels, where he had another fruitful ministry getting to know everyone, from the 'boots' and kitchen maids to the managers and managing directors. He was a wonderful priest, with the most pastoral of hearts. When he invited me to preach for him, as I had done previously in Liverpool, he conducted the service with such joy and dignity that one felt it to be a true act of worship. Afterwards, one of the churchwardens, who was General Manager of the Great Western Railway, took us all out to lunch at the company hotel in Paddington, and presented me with a Great Western tie.

Back at Burrswood, one of Dorothy Kerin's 'girls', Kathleen Nest, who as a young violinist had played under the baton of Sir Edward Elgar at the Three Choirs Festival, fell ill and died. Anne and I had become very attached to her, and her death was a blow we felt keenly. While I was taking the funeral in the church of Christ the Healer, I began to have the strange feeling that our tent pegs were being loosened once again. This seemed very odd, since we were so happy at Burrswood and had made some very deep friendships, not least with Gareth and Mary Tuckwell. But after the service I discovered that Anne had felt the same thing. Yet again something had struck us simultaneously: we were sure it was God's will and that we must obey. It was curious that the church of Christ the Healer, which had been instrumental in our call to our present ministry, and in some ways to our living at Burrswood, should be the place where we were forewarned of our departure.

★   ★   ★

Anne and I were both sure where we had to go – Whitehill Chase. It was sad to have to share our conviction with the Tuckwells and other members of the community. But perhaps God was telling us that the Acorn headquarters should be built up further and the training of members of the Apostolate transferred there? Both sets of Trustees were in agreement and pleased (we thought) about our move, as were David and Dorothy Smethurst, who would still be in charge of the house at Whitehill.

We began to pack up and, as a joke, hired the nearby 'Bishop's Move' removal firm: Gareth and others took photographs of us posing by the van! Johanna Ernst kindly supplied us all with cups of tea and nibbles throughout the day, and it was a good thing that she, an ex-nurse, was on hand, because one of the men knocked himself out on a low beam in the porch. It took a little time for him to recover. I recall that for the first three weeks I had worn a hat to prevent myself doing just the same thing.

Our grateful farewells said, we set off for Whitehill Chase. Some time earlier, the Trustees had been so encouraged by the work the Smethursts were doing that they had voted to develop the centre, and our arrival coincided with the completion of the major works set in hand. There was a fine new chapel, octagonal in shape and full of light, with a tiny side chapel for private prayer which Anne and I were to furnish in memory of our parents. The stable block now had eight bedrooms, attractively furnished with input from Dorothy, while David's practical experience had been invaluable in overseeing the work. He had acquired and renovated a wooden bungalow, and as Anne and I had decided that we should build our own home in the grounds with the money we had received from the sale of our Salisbury property, kindly offered this to us as temporary accommodation. The main house had new bathrooms, one accessible for disabled people, or 'differently abled' as Trevor Nash always liked to say. The kitchens were modernized and a dining room built on, while the drawing room and dining room of the old house were converted into a fair-sized conference room which could be divided by folding doors. There was also a library on the way to the chapel where our books were sold, as well as an office/storeroom, four bedrooms and two rooms for offices. The west wing, where David and Dorothy had a flat, was also refurbished. It all looked very smart, and now with 16 bedrooms in total (there were four in the bungalow), we would be able to hold fair-sized conferences or retreats.

We invited Princess Alexandra to formally declare the renovations and additions 'open', and when she arrived, on a glorious summer's day, the two chairmen of Trustees introduced her to the Smethursts and the rest of the staff. With a smile and knowing look as Anne and I came forward, she said, 'We have met before' – which we had, in Cambridge and York. She was most interested to hear of the progress of Acorn, visibly pleased with all that had been done on the campus, and glad to chat to the crowd of workers and Acorn members.

The following day, Lord and Lady Coggan (as they became in retirement) came over so that Donald could bless the work and dedicate the chapel. Afterwards we processed 'properly dressed', as Dean Milner-White would have said, to a marquee on the lawn where everyone could be accommodated, and had a short service followed by a reception. It was another lovely occasion – the Coggans were both in good form, and Anne was glad to have a deep chat with Jean.

Having settled into the bungalow, we began discussing the building of our new home with James More-Molyneux of Loseley Park. When James came home from the war, he had found his house in a parlous state and immediately began making blocks for the building industry to earn some money. His interest in the industry grew and gradually he was able to found and build up a company he named Guildway, which specialized in upmarket prefabricated housing. At the same time his secretary had begun making cottage cheese from the separated milk of their special herd of Jersey cows, and eventually Loseley Park Farms, makers of the famous ice cream and other delicacies, came into being. With these two industries up and running, James was able to renovate his house and estate and manage its upkeep.

We looked with him at plans for the sort of house we required, and when it became settled, James kindly put us in touch with two people he was happy to recommend for the building – John and his son Mark. They proved an excellent choice.

The site for the house was not so easily resolved. We spent some time trying to agree a location with the Whitehill Trustees, who decided they would prefer if it were not visible from the main building. (Had they seen the house once it was built, they might have felt differently, for John fashioned the brickwork and roof to be completely in keeping with the other buildings.) Eventually we had to settle for a site on the edge of a wood, near the stable block and just off the drive. This initial disappointment was alleviated as the footings went in and the building began to rise. John was most co-operative and consulted us at every turn, inviting us to choose the layout of each room (which, being prefabricated, was flexible) and all the furnishings and fittings. On the ground floor we had a large drawing room, a decent-sized dining room, a fine kitchen with utility room and a downstairs cloakroom off a small hall. The kitchen was one we had seen in a shop in Alton with a yellow and white theme. The shop owner was a local churchwarden and generously gave us an 'ecclesiastical discount'! Upstairs there was a large bedroom with ensuite and built-in wardrobes, my study, our chapel and a second bathroom. (We were able to accommodate in the stable block any visitors who came to stay.) James and Sue More-Molyneux kindly gave us the porch, and we made a small garden in the front with the help of Ken and Joan Littlefield, members of the Whitehill Chase team in which Ken was the sacristan.

Anne had her eightieth birthday while the house was being built – on 23 October 1991 – but was still working flat out. In fact, we were in it by Christmas, delighted with everything and glad to show our appreciation at a joyful opening celebration to John, Mark and the other men who had been involved. Lord and Lady Coggan came over from Winchester once again for the occasion, and Donald robed and blessed the house before the party.

Back at work, we undertook a number of trips, first to the Roman Catholic Metropolitan Cathedral in Liverpool, with its unique funnel-shaped centrepiece. I had been invited to preach and help with the ministry at a healing service one Sunday afternoon, and at lunch beforehand with the administrator and his fellow priests, Anne was asked what she would like to drink. When she requested a sherry, I saw the faces of the company drop slightly, and it was only after much hunting through cupboards that one priest, with a loud cry, finally emerged triumphant with a bottle. We had not been warned they only drank gin!

Though the music at the service was glorious, preaching was a little difficult because the shape of the cathedral, famously built in the round, meant that people were sitting across a wide spectrum. However, we all enjoyed a fine act of worship and ministry, and afterwards Anne and I were shown around by the Administrator. We were thrilled to find one of the chapels dedicated to the Three Oils – of healing, baptism and confirmation.

Crossing the Pennines, we arrived in Bradford where we had been invited to stay at the cathedral vicarage with John and Sue Richardson. John wanted us to meet his chapter, his healing team and churchwardens and to preach at a healing service in the Anglican cathedral. The ministry was obviously going well, and his team were in good heart – John was always a man of ideas and vision.

After a spell at home we set off for the West Country where (Lord) Raymond Hylton, our Trustee, had arranged for me to preach in his cathedral at Clifton, Bristol. It was good to see him and Joanna at Ammerdown again, and to meet some of their family.

Again the cathedral was not easy to preach in because one spoke from the centre, with the congregation stretched over 180°. It was a case of keeping one's mouth near the microphone, while looking far over to the right and left, rather like at Christ Church, Oxford. The Bishop of Clifton himself came to preside, an impressive man to whom I warmed. He and I blessed the team of ministrants and then prayed while the ministry proceeded. The organ was played by their fourth musician, who was brilliant. Again it was all dignified and an inspiring act of worship.

On 25 January 1992, St Paul's Day, Donald and Jean Coggan, together with John Yates who was now head of staff at Lambeth, came over for a Eucharist in the chapel. It was the 36th anniversary of Donald's consecration, and the 20th of John's and mine. Donald celebrated, attended by John and me on either side, while Anne played the organ. Several Acorn friends, staff and Trustees attended, and the Whitehill Chase staff managed to lunch us all afterwards. We reminisced about Beverley 20 years ago, while Donald told us about his consecration to Bradford and York Minster in 1956, just at the time of the interregnum between Cyril Garbett and Michael Ramsey. The day was one of great thanksgiving.

Gatherings of new Apostolate members and courses to train Christian Listeners were becoming a regular feature of life at Whitehill Chase, while David and Dorothy had formed a team of mostly local people to assist with the growing ministry at the Tuesday Eucharists. David had a brief for the four contiguous dioceses of Winchester, Guildford, Portsmouth and Chichester. He was also developing the office and the kitchen staff, while we were very fortunate to have the services of Terry, a fine Christian, as gardener and general factotum. From time to time, people on six-month placements would join in the life of the Chase and assist Terry – people such as Simon Newitt who subsequently went into business, and Phelim McIntyre who became assistant manager of the SPCK shop in Chichester. We enjoyed having friends to stay, such as John Simpson and John Manchester, and our cousin Helen on her occasional trips south. All the time, the developing work of Acorn kept us fully occupied, as we met frequently with the Trustees and staff and continued our travels.

Chapter 10

More changes and our last move

At the beginning of Eastertide 1992, a surprise letter arrived which afforded us much joy. The Bishop of Chichester, Eric Kemp, wrote to invite me to become a canon in his cathedral with the prebendal stall of Bracklesham. We had been attending Sunday worship whenever we were able to do so, and were thrilled that one of us would once more be on the foundation of the cathedral where we had been married.

The installation was fixed for May in the context of Evensong. After the oaths of allegiance and the Bishop's mandate and blessing, the procedure was that the new canon was presented with a small loaf of bread. This was the token of his living which was supplied by the prebend in the old days – in this case Bracklesham parish, the church of which is now sadly under the sea. The parish, however, continues as St Anne's, East Wittering and includes Bracklesham Bay. The new canon was also given a rod or rule to remind him of the statutes of the cathedral which he had promised to obey, and a copy of the Bible by the Dean to show him it was the word of God he was bound to proclaim. It was a good and enjoyable service with excellent music, and Anne and I felt supported by the presence of Cocky and Joan Trower (from Stansteadbury, on their way to his SAS reunion), James and Sue More-Molyneux, and Charles and Anita Longbottom, among others. The Dean, John Treadgold,

135

and his wife Hazel, with whom we were to begin a long and happy friendship, generously held a reception for us all in the Deanery afterwards. We really felt part of our beloved cathedral again.

The duties of a canon were minimal but I had the joy of the annual chapter meeting and dinner, the latter still being extended to canons *emeriti*. Later on in retirement I was able to take a turn in preaching, celebrating the Eucharist, reading lessons and even, in the absence of the priest vicar, singing Evensong.

The year also saw encouraging visits to other cathedrals, including Leicester and Southwark, and we felt privileged to minister in Westminster Abbey, the church at the heart of our nation, where the canon who was in charge of education and outreach had arranged regular services of healing as part of the Abbey's life and witness. Anne and I had a far-reaching talk with him and those who had taken part over lunch. We also returned to Canterbury, where Archbishop Runcie, Dame Cicely Saunders, Dr Kenneth Leese and I had all contributed to a week of lectures on health and healing in the cathedral a few years previously. In response, the diocese had set up a healing panel, and great strides had been made in advancing the ministry in the parishes of the diocese. When I preached in the cathedral, the service was so well attended that we felt assured that the ministry of healing was making a significant impact in the Primate of All England's own diocese. All dioceses now, in fact, had advisers in place; there was a real hope that the Christian Healing Ministry was genuinely taking root.

The next year, 1993, it seemed appropriate to choose York, the place from which Acorn had sprung, as the venue for the conference to mark its tenth year – and my tenth year in the office of Adviser to the Archbishops. After a Eucharist of Thanksgiving in the Minster, we gathered at St

John's College (now the College of Ripon and York St John). Many had made the journey from the south, and it was also good to have John Manchester with us again, his parish of Old Malton only being half an hour away. The daily morning talks given by Bishop Michael Marshall, who was at his most inspiring best, were the highlight of the conference. Aware of what had been achieved in the churches during the past ten years, he gave us a vision for the future and encouraged us to enter the next decade with the same enthusiasm that had motivated us up to this point. Everyone was grateful for his ministry and his stimulating message. Another blessing to the conference was the integration of the two themes of our work – the Apostolate and Christian Listeners. Discussion groups and meals provided the opportunity for cross-fertilization and joint planning, and increased our fellowship and friendship.

On the last day, we took our witness out to the city, with many churches holding services and teaching sessions. It was heartening to see a good number of our Northern Prayer Fellowship who had brought friends to these gatherings. For the final service in the city, Russ Parker ministered alongside Anne and myself. He had now been appointed our deputy.

We returned to Yorkshire in the autumn for what turned out to be a nostalgic trip down memory lane. John Simpson returned from Australia to celebrate the 25th anniversary of his ordination to the priesthood at St Martin-on-the-Hill, Scarborough, and John Manchester came to assist at the Eucharist while I preached. In my sermon I related how Donald Coggan, who had been impressed by both Johns at their ordination interviews, had remarked, 'Morris, you do collect real characters.' At the end of the service I was about to give the blessing when John Simpson interrupted, 'Not yet, Bishop!' and called Anne up from the congregation. She was presented with an enormous bouquet of flowers as a 'Thank you' for all she had done for him when we were together in Scarborough. After meeting old friends and parishioners, and the exhaustive taking of photographs, many of us repaired to John Manchester's vicarage in Old Malton where he had kindly provided lunch. Before returning home we had a meeting of our healing prayer fellowship, which Leslie Stanbridge and Maurice Pettitt had so lovingly kept together.

We had another visit to Portsmouth Cathedral the following year for the diocesan healing day. Richard Eckersley, an old Trinity and Chichester friend, had done much to forward the healing ministry while he was a Canon Residentiary, and has continued to spearhead this ministry, even 15 years after his retirement. In this he has been ably assisted by Peg Price, who has organized the annual days in the cathedral for many years, which have been manifestly of great blessing in the diocese and done much to forward the work in that part of the country.

Back in the summer of 1993 we were able to set up a joint scheme with Chichester Theological College. Peter Atkinson had recently become Principal – in later years as Chancellor of the cathedral, he would actually be our next-door neighbour – and on his staff was Brother Reginald SSF, who was keen that the students should have some experience of ministry during their training. Accordingly, he arranged for parties of students to come to Whitehill Chase from time to time for a day of instruction, and also for two students at a time to have a placement with us. The first two were excellent and appreciative, one now being an archdeacon in the diocese (Philip Jones), the other ministering in the Church in Wales. But after a year or two, the scheme sadly came to a sudden end with the closure of the college.

*   *   *

The past months had seen some staff changes. To our sadness, the Trustees felt they could no longer afford a full-time administrator, and so Nigel Beazley, who had endeared himself to all workers and members of the staff and been a great help to Anne and me personally, had to leave us. Additionally, David and Dorothy Smethurst, who had done so much to make Whitehill Chase a going concern, were called to a parish in Epsom. We set about trying to replace all three as best we could.

We were fortunate in finding a part-time administrator in the person of Jamie Jamieson, who had actually been station commander at Gatow aerodrome in Berlin, shortly after my tour of duty in 1948. After retiring from the RAF, Jamie had worked in York, where we had met him and his wife Gwen. Now he was to retire to Farnham, just a few miles north of Whitehill Chase. Gwen and Jamie began coming to the centre regularly, and eventually the Trustees invited him to take the post of part-time administrator. It was a blessing for us to have them nearby.

It was not so easy to find the right warden and wife to replace David and Dorothy. After advertising, we shortlisted four, of whom two were obviously front runners. Then it became difficult. The Trustees and a member of staff wanted one candidate, while we wanted the other who had been one of my parish priests in York. In fact the first candidate had alienated the office staff before the interviews even began, which Anne and I deemed did not augur well. Sadly, we could not come to an agreement and so we had to advertise again.

The second time we were much more fortunate. Canon Stephen Sidebotham, who had been Dean of Hong Kong, and his wife Peggy had applied for the job and we were all agreed they should come. It proved to be completely the right choice and a real blessing. Stephen, who with his wisdom and wholesome spirituality was gifted with joinery and DIY skills, and Peggy, whose boundless energy paid dividends in the garden, house and bookshop, quickly endeared themselves to staff and visitors alike. They were both experienced in the ministry of healing, and Stephen was a good member of the team, teaching at the conferences and also instructing those who ministered with him at the Tuesday services. They were also wonderful neighbours to Anne and me on the campus.

The year 1994 was to be fruitful as we consolidated the work, seeing that it always had an outward thrust. It was also the year we had to think about retirement. I considered it would be a good compromise to retire when I was about 67½, halfway between the voluntary age (65) and the compulsory age (70), in the autumn of 1995. We had always believed that we would remain in the house we had built, thinking it would serve as an excellent retirement home. But we began to consider that we might be very much on our own, because we would not want to interfere with our successor or with the work after we had left.

It was on one of our Sunday visits to Chichester that I casually asked Canon John Hester, the Precentor, whether any houses in the Close ever became available. I had known John in my theatre chaplaincy days, when he was at St Paul's Covent Garden and acted as our 'Archdeacon'. He replied that there were in fact two apartments coming up and suggested that I write to John Treadgold, the Dean. John invited us down for a talk with himself and the Communar, Captain Michael Shallow RN – the senior lay administrator on the cathedral staff. There were two possibilities, one of which had just become vacant, the other currently occupied. We asked if we could see the vacant one, and Michael Shallow showed us round. It was half of the Chantry, a fine thirteenth-century house with a twelfth-century porch which had been the undercroft of the Chanters' chapel. One entered through a panelled hall into a beautiful drawing room with a door into the garden. Through what had been the green baize door when it was all one house, there was a fine parquet-floored dining room, a breakfast room (with another door into the garden) a kitchen and a downstairs cloakroom. Upstairs there were four bedrooms (one being a very large main bedroom), a bathroom and good cupboard space. It was love at first sight! We gratefully accepted the Dean's offer, agreed to the rent and began to make arrangements, the Dean and Chapter kindly offering to put in central heating for which we would pay half. We learned that the house would be ready by Christmas, and after various consultations with the Acorn Trustees, agreed to move in on 22 December to avoid a long vacancy which the Dean and Chapter naturally did not want. We would complete our last eight months of work from Chichester.

Meanwhile, the autumn work was upon us. That autumn I had two preachments in Cambridge colleges. At Girton, famously established as the first residential college for women, we were surprised to find that 68 per cent of the undergraduates were men! I recalled that a surgeon friend in Scarborough had distinguished himself by being the father of the first male undergraduate to be admitted, while another friend had the similar distinction by having a daughter who was the first female undergraduate at Trinity. When Anne and I arrived at Girton we were offered the hospitality of the house and felt very much welcomed, but Anne was a little disconcerted to find that she was shown to a 'mixed bathing' establishment. By then everyone in the college took such arrangements for granted.

We were also invited to Sidney Sussex College, where the chaplain had arranged for us to stay the night and we were able to see something of both common rooms. The service, though voluntary, was very well attended and the under-graduates certainly listened before joining us at a reception afterwards. Many were grateful that I had given personal examples, such as the healing of our verger in Scarborough, to illustrate what I was trying to say, and asked us both about our life and healing ministry. We then dined in hall with members of the senior common room who were equally charming, though by this time in our lives seemed very young indeed! We both greatly enjoyed ourselves, and the following morning had the luxury of being served breakfast in our suite of rooms. After visits to Heffers and Trinity we wended our way home, stopping to stay with the Trowers at Stansteadbury en route.

Those last months of 1994 were full, as we tried to build up the life of our Acorn headquarters at Whitehill Chase and further shape the team. We made appearances at the increasing number of conferences, as well as the regular staff meetings, now always at the Chase, and the Trustees' meetings, usually in London. In our spare time we had to turn our attention to planning our move – moves always seem to entail much sorting out and turning out, however short the time one has lived in the house! We felt some pangs at the prospect of leaving the home we had built for ourselves only three years earlier and at leaving Stephen and Peggy, the other occupants of the site, who had become great friends. There was also in the background the knowledge that this was leading to retirement, the laying down of our lives' work. We cheered our spirits with the thought that we were in a sense going home: not only would we live under the shadow of our beloved cathedral, but next door to the house in which we had had our wedding reception.

Indeed, there was much work going on at the Chichester end. The Chapter had now kindly decided to decorate the house right through for us, since the previous occupants had lived in it for 25 years. They suggested we choose colours with the painters, and told us we were welcome to come and measure up whenever we wanted. We managed to get down most Sundays for the Sung Eucharist, after which we usually lunched in the Dolphin, the hotel opposite the cathedral. Conveniently, the Dolphin was offering cheap five-day breaks for Christmas shoppers just at the time we were due to move, so we booked to stay there for the duration.

In our last days at Whitehill Chase we were greatly touched by the helpfulness of Stephen and Peggy and the staff, especially Terry, the genial Christian gardener. After saying some sad farewells to them, the removal firm loaded two vans with our belongings and we set off. We had particularly engaged this firm from Bognor because they had a van low enough to drive under the Canon Lane archway. To their great disappointment, it broke down, and when, as arranged, we met them at 7 a.m. the following morning, we found a pantechnicon parked outside in South Street. The poor men had to carry everything, including Anne's Steinway, the 60 yards to our house. To my sympathetic remarks, the boss replied, 'It'll do our muscles good.'

Their muscles certainly were tested, for Anne's sitting room and my study were to be upstairs in two of the bedrooms. That meant that my four-decker filing cabinet (full), innumerable boxes of books and the furniture (our bedroom fittings were oak) had to be carried up 17 fairly steep stairs. The men managed it all without a mishap.

Following the Dorothy Kerin tradition of booking the bishop as a stimulus to making sure the work was completed by the time he turned up, we had arranged for Bishop Eric to come to bless the house on the feast of the Epiphany, 6 January. As it was now 22 December, we had to set to work with some urgency. We went to bed tired every night and had to send out a 'Come over to Macedonia' call to Stephen and Peggy, who joined us for a day in the New Year. While Stephen put up the light fittings, bookshelves, curtain rails and the like, Peggy unpacked boxes, helped by Pam Boyd, a friend in the congregation. Gradually our half of the beautiful Chantry, which was such a fine setting for our possessions, was transformed into a place of harmony and order. It was like returning home.

Chapter 11

Full circle:
Chichester and retirement

Within a few weeks, Anne and I had begun to settle into life in the Cathedral Close. We were both thrilled with the high standard of music under the expert direction of Alan Thurlow (we had been present at his first Sunday in the cathedral in 1980 during the celebrations for our Silver Wedding). He and his wife Tina lived at 2 St Richard's Walk, which had also been the organist's house in Anne's day. His very competent assistant organist, James Thomas, and James's organist wife Katharine, lived nearby in Canon Lane. Also in Canon Lane was the Deanery (occupied by John and Hazel Treadgold), the Archdeaconry (Michael and Daphne Brotherton), the Residentiary (John and Liz Hester, John being the Precentor) and the Chantry (the Manktelows and ourselves). Canon Roger Greenacre (the Chancellor) lived at 4 Vicar's Close, while David Nason (Priest Vicar) lived at 1 St Richard's Walk above Keith Masters (Second Verger) and his wife Julie. It was also good to find Bishop Edward Knapp-Fisher and his wife Joan at 2 Vicar's Close. Susan Evershed, daughter of Rupert Browne-Wilkinson who had married us, lived at 1 Vicar's Close, while Michael and Wendy Shallow lived at no. 3. Bishop Eric and his wife Pat resided in the Palace at the far end of Canon Lane. Peter Kellett (Head Verger) and his wife Jane also lived in Canon Lane and were, like others, most helpful and caring to us. It was a joy too to have the

Lay Vicars in the precincts. The cathedral community in the Close (along with Frank Hawkins the Treasurer and his wife Gillian who lived outside) proved to be a truly Christian fellowship of friends.

As Anne and I immersed ourselves in the steady round of daily Choral Evensong, sung Eucharist on Sundays, and regular celebration of the Eucharist in our chapel (we had converted an alcove off our large bedroom into an oratory), we began to feel again the quiet, loving embrace of the Lord. We were slowing down from a life of always being on the go. No longer living at the hub of the Acorn work meant an easing of the pressure and a chance to recharge our batteries: there was more time to read, to think and to pray, as well as to enjoy each other's company. I was thrilled to see Anne's happiness at being in the milieu she loved and knew so well.

We had a sizeable garden to look after, which was a complete joy. The house opened on to a terrace, overlooking a large lawn stretching right up to the city wall. (We quickly purchased a good motor mower.) There were a few apple trees, a big rose bed, and a fine old mulberry, blown down in the 1987 storm, but still continuing to bear abundant fruit from its recumbent position on the ground. Anne suggested that we put in variegated shrubs which would brighten up the winter months, and over the years we counted that we had planted 37! Stephen and Peggy kindly came over from Whitehill Chase to help us clear some of the ground, and on one occasion Peggy was so over-enthusiastic in tending her bonfire that some of the South Street windows were filled with smoke. An irate inhabitant came and lectured me at the front door, brushing aside my apologies and demanding to know my name! David Graebe gave us four excellent rhododendrons from his fine garden at Chant Stream Cottage, and more plants were brought by other friends, visits from those near and far being quite a feature in our lives from this time on. Happily, we also saw more of our cousins, Sue and her family in Heyshott, and Helen on Hayling Island.

I was glad to be able to be more supportive of Bishop Eric and the Chapter now too. Having done a minimum amount during my eight years as an assistant bishop and three as a canon, I now found myself helping at confirmations, healing days and services, and taking a turn preaching in the cathedral. The only sadness around this time was the order by General Synod of the closure of our beloved theological college, the oldest in the country. The scheme of teaching ordinands at Whitehill Chase was suddenly stopped (as mentioned earlier) only a year or two after we had initiated it, while the loss to Chichester, to the cathedral and, I believe, to the Church of England as a whole, was great. The Principal, Peter Atkinson, was suddenly out of a job and the staff put in limbo. Bishop Eric looked after Peter of course, and after three years as Vicar of Lavant, he was appointed Chancellor of the cathedral before becoming Dean of Worcester.

Most of our remaining eight months at Acorn were spent preparing for the annual meeting – this year (1995) in Birmingham – which would be our last while in office. What topic should I take as the theme of my address? As I prayed about this, the subject that kept coming to mind was the danger of fundamentalism. I felt that to purvey a faith that was fenced round by prejudices and inhibitions was a negation of the Holy Spirit. Of course, a 'charismatic' free-for-all can also have its blind spots: what I believed was needed was an obedient listening to the Spirit within, the disciplined reading of scripture and partaking in the liturgy, in order that we might point the way to God's kingdom wherever we have been called to serve him. These thoughts were to become the substance of my address at the conference.

Indeed, the dangers of straying from this spiritual discipline have become apparent in the present situation in the Anglican Communion.

We were very moved by the large attendance at the conference (it was noted that James More-Molyneux had been at every one!). As always, worship occupied centre stage, but there were stimulating talks too, and we were given plenty of time for fellowship. Little did Anne and I anticipate how the event was to end – with a very special 'This is your Life'! Charles Longbottom, assuming the mantle of Eamonn Andrews, called on members of the staff and Apostolate – including John Manchester from Scarborough days, and June Hall, my secretary in York – to say a few words, which inevitably led to a certain amount of teasing at our expense. Then came an even greater surprise. Charles and his colleagues had smuggled into the college the two people who had had the greatest influence on us both – Donald and Jean Coggan! We were astonished beyond measure as we greeted them. Questioned by Charles, Donald, with his bubbling sense of fun, continued the leg-pulling and said some very kind things. The whole event was a joy and took away some of the sadness we felt at saying farewell to the many friends who had worked so devotedly with us. Retirement brings its sorrows with its joys (2 Corinthians 6.10).

*   *   *

September brought our Ruby Wedding and a trip up to Yorkshire where our friends, Richard and Virginia Storey of Settrington, had offered to host a black-tie event, suggesting we choose the guests. Joy Howard-Vyse, now in her ninetieth year, gave a lift to Anne Brooksbank; David and Ursula Westbury came from Malton, bringing John Manchester and John Simpson; Martin and Bridget Fitzalan-Howard came from near York, while Mick and Lucy Willoughby, three of whose children I had baptized, drove over from North Grimston on the edge of the Wolds. It was a delightful party, with the ladies looking resplendent in their evening dresses. After dinner, to our utter surprise, Richard presented us with a painting. As we unwrapped it, we wondered if it might be York Minster, but no, it was a large and very fine watercolour of Chichester Cathedral. Unbeknown to us, Richard and Virginia had paid a visit to Sussex and commissioned the work from a local, well-known marine artist Bob McKay. The watercolour now hangs in the thirteenth-century hall of our house and is much admired by all who come to visit us. On either side hang twin Portuguese carvings, possibly eighteenth century. One depicts the lifting up of the serpent for healing in the wilderness, the other Jesus the Son of Man lifted up on the cross for the healing of the world (John 3.14). We were fortunate to buy them for a pound each in an antique shop, soon after we were married.

Christmas Day was the final 'celebration' of the year. After the most glorious sung Eucharist, with magnificent music and ceremonial, we repaired to John and Liz Hester's home for Christmas dinner. Liz was the envy of many people because she had no idea of time. If the sun was in the right position she might well go out and paint, and the drawing room functioned as her studio. Her youngest son Alex used to take bets from the congregation as to what time his dear mother would serve up Christmas dinner. And being a true artist, when she did serve it, we were treated to a magnificent feast with all the trimmings.

For a Christmas present that year, I gave Anne a small enamel box for her earrings inscribed '1995 – a year to remember'. It was.

★　　★　　★

In the following months, several friends began asking if I would write another book, but at the time I did not feel moved to do so. I wanted to enjoy my retirement with Anne, and in any case I was somewhat weary. I recalled how Donald Coggan had said that he slept for the first six months after retiring. It was also curious, I reflected, that I had produced all six of my books when I was exceptionally busy and immersed in work. Perhaps it needed such a stimulus. In fact, it would be ten years before I wrote again.

Holy Week, when the ceremonies of each day were solemnized with gravity and devotion, was a time to experience in the cathedral. The Altar of Repose and the Watch – which reminded us of our days at St Martin-on-the-Hill – and the Easter Garden, were all beautiful and moving, while the sung Eucharist on Easter Day, with brass accompanying the organ and dignified but not over-fussy ceremonial, was the Church of England liturgy seen and heard at its best.

Frequently on Easter Day we were invited to lunch with Michael and Daphne at the Archdeaconry; they generously entertained on this occasion those who had no family or lived on their own.

The first month of 1997 contained another anniversary: it was 25 years since my consecration in Beverley Minster, and planning for this occasion had already begun in the previous year. John Treadgold suggested I should celebrate a sung Eucharist for which the cathedral choir would be present, and Bishop Eric agreed to come and preside from his throne. It was obvious that the person who should preach was Archbishop Donald. Next we made a list of those we should invite, and as the replies came in we began to wonder how we were going to accommodate and entertain everyone – about 130 in all. Would it be possible to have the Tudor Room in the Palace? It was kind and generous of Pat Kemp to agree to this and offer the use of her kitchen. Now, what about the caterers? We went to pick the brains of Peter and Jane Kellett. To our amazement, Jane suddenly said, 'I will do it.' We knew she presided over a most hospitable house, where we were regular guests, but she admitted that she had never previously catered for so many. However, when Jane says 'Yes', her determination, like Anne's, takes over. With a great amount of planning, the meal was cooked in stages, and stored in our and others' freezers. Jane and Peter did not stop there: they organized the tables and chairs, but saw that the maximum we could seat in the Tudor room was 70. We therefore decided to divide our guests into two halves. Luncheon for 70, including all who came from afar, would be served on the day, while the 60 guests who lived in or near Chichester would be invited to supper on the Sunday night. Jane was to keep a record of all her costs, including the wine we bought at bulk prices, so that we could reimburse her in full. Unbeknown to us, she also organized flowers, not only for the tables but also for Jean Coggan, Pat Kemp and Anne.

The next step was to go and see Alan Thurlow about the music. He kindly allowed us to choose the whole service, including the hymns, some of which would commemorate St Paul, since it was of course the feast of his conversion. Rather unambitiously we chose 'Darke in F' as the setting because Harold Darke had been a friend of Anne's in her Chichester days. Later on it would have been the Widor or Vierne's Mass. For the anthem, we naturally asked for *Expectans Expectavi*. Although in the cathedral music library, the piece was not in current use, and Alan was glad to reintroduce it to the repertoire. The previous evening James Thomas kindly went through the part in which I sang the liturgy, and Peter Kellet the ceremonial.

Shortly before the service on the day, Donald Coggan telephoned us from the middle of a traffic jam on the notorious

A27 to say he would be late. David Nason and Keith Masters were deputed to welcome and look after him, and to bring Jean up to sit with Anne. The Coggans arrived just as we were beginning to process in and I was able to break briefly from the precession to say hello. David and Keith were obviously anxious, but Donald was completely at peace and told them there was plenty of time before the sermon. They came in during the Gradual.

As always, Donald preached a compelling sermon. He spoke with authority, and the choristers were especially alert and said later they had never heard such a voice before. A great number of Acorn staff and members and many friends were present. John Simpson and John Manchester had come down specially and together conducted the intercessions and concelebrated with five other Bishops, Mark Green, Michael Marshall, Lindsay Bishop of Horsham, Michael Manktelow and Christopher Luxmore, and of course the Dean and Chapter. The music was magnificent. I wore the white chasuble Anne had made for me in Helperthorpe days and my Acorn (blue) mitre made by Helen Walker, an Acorn doctor.

Afterwards, Jane produced her excellent luncheon. At our table with the Coggans we had some of our mutual York friends, Mark Green and David and Dorothy Blunt. Dorothy was by now in a wheelchair, and we were delighted that David had managed to bring her for the occasion. Several people came to 'tea' afterwards and found that champagne was on the menu! On the Sunday evening, Jane undertook her second marathon as we entertained the musicians, several of the local people, and John May, still head server at St Martin-on-the-Hill, who had been crucifer at the service and had travelled down with Hazel McWhan and Pam Humble. Daphne Brotherton kindly put them up. It was a happy gathering, and Anne and I greatly enjoyed the celebration. Later in 1997 we made our pilgrimage back to Beverley Minster, where I preached at a service of thanksgiving.

The following years saw our increasing involvement with the Chichester Cathedral Choristers' Association (CCCA). Anne had been elected a full member of the Association and I had been chosen as honorary chaplain. We were glad to get to know the boy choristers and gentlemen of the choir a little better, and also to care for the old choristers. At the annual meeting, Alan would invite them to join with the choir in singing the anthem at Evensong, and afterwards Anne and I would have everyone, including the organists and lay vicars, for wine in our garden. It made a happy ending to the day.

The eve of 2000 saw us at a well-attended service in the cathedral, conducted by the Dean, John Treadgold. It was a special time, thanking God for the past and dedicating ourselves afresh to him for what was to come. We continued to enjoy receiving guests, some from overseas like John Simpson, whose annual visits from Australia were a delight, always filled with laughter. In September 2000, the time of our 45th wedding anniversary, we were glad to welcome David Storey, a doctor from Toronto, and his wife Anne. Nearly ten years previously, they had brought a party to Burrswood, where we had heard about their hope of building and running a place like Burrswood in Canada. They planned a Christian hospital with Christian staff where Christ the Healer would be at the centre of their work. On their return they began to raise the money, and the hospital opened early in the new millennium (around the time of their visit to us in Chichester). It proved to be a success, helping and inspiring many people. After about five years, however, funds seemed to dry up. As we had found in Acorn, it was crucial to have people who raised a steady income, and a hard-working staff. It seems nothing short of a tragedy that such an enterprise in Christian mission and healing has not survived.

⋆   ⋆   ⋆

The great event of 2001 for us was Anne's 90th birthday party. Many people had not realized her age and were somewhat surprised when they received their invitations! The evening began at Evensong, where, at Anne's request, Alan Thurlow kindly had Charles Wood's service in D and, of course, *Expectans Expectavi*. James Thomas, now organist and master of the choristers at Bury St Edmunds Cathedral, gave an improvisation that began with the opening chords of the Poulenc Organ Concerto. It was a brilliant *tour de force*. There followed an organ recital in which Alan played two movements (I and IV) of Widor's Fifth Symphony; Mark Wardell, who had succeeded James as assistant organist, played Vierne's first movement from his Sixth Symphony and Bach's St Anne Fugue; and the organ scholar Edmund Aldhouse played one of Vierne's 24 pieces and César Franck's Chorale No. 3. The worship and the recital made a glorious beginning to the night.

We then adjourned to the Vicars' Hall for supper with quite a large company for whom Jane Kellett had catered with accustomed expertise. Anne and I received our guests, who were very generous with their presents, before finding ourselves seated – in Anne's honour – with all the cathedral organists and their wives, Bishop Eric and Pat, John and Hazel Treadgold, the Chapter and the lay vicars. The newly arrived Communar, David Mowlam and his wife Kay, sat with my cousin Helen. Geoffrey Barnard, now Anne's friend of 63 years, made a very amusing speech, reminiscing about their early days as pupils together and visits to Paris organ lofts, before proposing her health. During coffee, Anne, who had told me nothing of her intentions, stood up amid cheers to thank Geoffrey and everyone else for coming, Jane for the catering, and the musicians for all they had contributed to the evening. She said we could all do with a great deal more of such excellent music performed to this high standard, and received a great ovation. Our neighbours kindly gave us a hand back home with all the presents.

Helen was over again at Christmas, bringing my first cousin Andrew. He had been in the Secret Service as head of the German/Austrian branch during and after the war, and had come to see me in Berlin. He poignantly wrote in our visitors' book, 'Too long absence since we last met. Must do better in coming year.' He died soon afterwards. Helen, however, recorded that we had 'A jolly luncheon together'. It was a happy last memory of a dear cousin.

Anniversaries for both of us were opportunities for great thanksgiving, and 25 January 2002 brought another milestone as I completed the third decade of my episcopate. I was able to celebrate the Eucharist and robe for Evensong, with, as always, a good lunch in between. John Manchester came down on his post-Christmas break. It began quite a year of entertaining many friends and family.

We then had the sadness of saying our goodbyes to Donald Coggan, who had moved into a nursing home near Winchester. He told me before he died, at the age of 90, that he had put my name up for a Lambeth DD but it had been turned down. The Archbishop awarded me the Cross of St Augustine instead.

Donald's funeral was a low-key occasion in his parish church, taken by his sensitive parish priest. His humility shone through even in death. Six weeks later, we gathered in Winchester Cathedral for a memorial service. Before it began, I went over to congratulate John Perry on the production of the report, *A Time to Heal*, which strongly commended the

Christian healing ministry to all the dioceses and parishes. It was full of excellent suggestions as to how to attain this purpose. His reply came unexpectedly: 'Morris, this is a commendation of your ministry.'

There was a good representation of bishops, headed by the Archbishop of Canterbury, clergy and lay people at the service. After the blessing, in a moving gesture, the Archbishop invited Jean to walk with him in the procession, while the Bishop of Winchester accompanied Ann, the elder daughter, and the Dean the younger one, Ruth. We joined a fine gathering of Donald's friends afterwards at the reception that Jean had laid on for us all. She died two years later. A devoted couple, they had been wonderful friends and mentors to us.

Visitors continued to come during the following years, and though we were able to get to the cathedral every day and go out regularly for lunch either at Park House in Bepton or the Millstream in Bosham – at both hotels we had made many friendships with the staff and management – the pace inevitably slowed down during 2003/4. After all, Anne was 92! But 2005 brought more celebrations. Trinity Sunday was the 50th anniversary of my ordination to the priesthood. Our thoughts inevitably went back to St Paul's Cathedral where we had sat so close to one another under the dome, and I received the sacrament of ordination from Bishop William Wand. These thoughts of thanksgiving permeated our hearts and minds that morning as we joined in the concelebrated sung Eucharist in the cathedral.

September brought our Golden Wedding. As the Park House dining-room table when fully extended only had 26 settings, we had some trouble drawing up the invitation list. Happily, our cousin Sue offered to put on a lunch for Anne's family in her home at Heyshott on the following Sunday.

For the first event, we tried to invite guests from every period of our lives: Geoffrey and Pat Barnard (Anne's early Chichester days), my cousin Helen, my god-daughter Susie (for whom I stood as godfather in Berlin in my Army days), John Simpson and John Manchester (Scarborough days), Peg Price, Charles and Anita Longbottom, Jamie and Gwen Jamieson (Acorn), Gareth Tuckwell (Burrswood), John and Hazel Treadgold, Jane Kellett and Jeremy Smith representing our Chichester friends, and Michael O'Brien, a friend of many years and owner of the hotel.

Many of Anne's relatives came to Sue's lunch on the Sunday, including Winifred (Anne's remaining first cousin), Cyril and Barbara Coomber, Don and Dot Quarmby, Peter and Maureen Christmas, and their daughters Joyce and Alison. It was a happy party.

Little did we know it would be the last time Anne would see all her family together.

Chapter 12

The testing years

Anne was in good health and on good form during all the celebrations, not least on her 90th birthday. We continued in our life of love and laughter, enjoying our visits to the cathedral each day, as well as our outings for lunch, and a drive about four times a week. But there had been a noticeable slowing down during 2005 and Anne was becoming a little frail.

In December she had a fall in the cloisters on the way back from Evensong. By then we were not only holding hands, but had our arms linked when walking. However, I could not hold her and she pulled me down, almost on top of her. A kind Prebendal schoolmaster helped us up.

I noticed a deterioration in Anne's health from that time, and as the summer of 2006 began it was obvious she was tiring as she prepared for the life of the world to come. I was already seeing to the cooking and day-to-day housework, but now helped her in getting up and dressing, and going to bed. Barry and Sheila Windsor, one of our doctor/nurse Acorn partnerships, came over from Bournemouth and took us out to lunch at Park House. By then the social services had kindly provided a wheelchair. The staff were distressed to see the deterioration in Anne, and it was to be our last visit there together, though a happy one.

Throughout the summer I was afraid of letting Anne fall

when she was getting in and out of bed and into the wheel-chair. A hospice nurse, Gina Ruff, graciously offered to lend a hand twice a week in the mornings, and eventually I had to employ a nursing service to help her twice a day. I also engaged the WRVS Meals on Wheels service, while Wendy Mitchell, who had helped me with the household duties twice a week for some years, continued to be a valuable support and friend.

To attend the cathedral, which by this time we were doing only on Sundays, we had to take the car. I drove Anne to the Treasury car park where one of the stewards on duty would kindly meet us and push her into the presbytery, near the High Altar. The sung Eucharist became a real highlight for us. I also celebrated each week at home and we received the reserved sacrament on the other days. By now Anne could hardly see, and I was reading to her, including the daily offices which we had always said together. The cathedral community was very warm and caring and we were conscious of their prayers.

By the beginning of September the nurses were finding their task very hard. The poor darling needed regular nursing and Sue Evershed-Martin, a friend from the cathedral who was on the committee of the Donnington Nursing Home only a mile away, managed to get Anne a bed there. She also booked the ambulance from the St John's organization. The hardest moment, which greatly moved me, was when Anne was carried out of our house. I realized it would be for the last time.

She settled quite happily into the nursing home which proved to be a first-rate choice. Not only was the nursing of a very high standard – all the senior staff had been ward sisters in the NHS – but the warm and prayerful caring (the matron and staff were Christians) had a beneficial effect on Anne. I was full of admiration and truly thankful. It was comforting to be able to see her every day, frequently assisting her with her meals, which in turn helped the nursing staff. The matron always came in for a chat and I was able to pray with Anne according to our usual custom.

Not long after Anne's arrival, we celebrated our 51st wedding anniversary. John Simpson was over from Australia, staying with Peter and Jane Kellett, and accompanied me to the nursing home that morning. He gave Anne a blessing with the laying on of hands, and offered a thanksgiving for our 51 years of marriage. Some time previously we had arranged that James and Sue More-Molyneux and Peg Price would all visit. I brought a bottle of champagne, Peg provided the glasses, and we had an unlooked-for and happy celebration in Anne's room. It became even more exciting when the staff brought in a large iced cake they had made! We shared it with our friends and all the staff, and at regular intervals a voice came from the bed – 'More please.' Anne really enjoyed our party and the champagne. I returned in the afternoon to be with her after James had generously taken the rest of us to the Millstream for lunch. The day left a beautiful glow.

The next day my lay-vicar neighbour, Jeremy, came to the nursing home to warn me that our house had been flooded after an exceptionally heavy torrent of rain. I returned home to find my bedroom saturated. Clare Feaver, a kindly neighbour, put me up.

About ten days later I had arranged to attend Julian Slade's memorial service at St Paul's, Covent Garden, and the nurses were quite hopeful this would be possible. Patricia Routledge had generously offered to take me in her car, being very understanding of the circumstances. However, when I went into the hospital at 9 a.m., the matron told me Anne's condition had worsened. I decided I must stay and briefly went home to ring Patricia and inform Tim

Schofield the Precentor of the situation. Tim was a musician and FRCO and had looked after Anne's spiritual welfare since his installation. Jeremy made arrangements to spend the whole day with me at the bedside – he had already been in to see Anne a few times, twice bringing John Mountford the organ scholar, who had asked to visit. It had always been touching to see how a younger generation of musicians loved and respected her.

It was 4 October, St Francis' Day, a saint Anne especially revered because of their mutual love of birds, the little folk. As Jeremy kept vigil with me, Tim came in twice, the second time to say the commendatory prayers. The matron and nurses paid regular visits, while Anne's cousin Sue sat with us the whole evening after work. Anne was so peaceful as her life gently ebbed away. I continued constantly to tell her how much I loved her, thanking her for being such a wonderful wife in every way and for all her love, and then praying for her with thanksgiving. At 10 p.m. she breathed her last. *Requiescat in pace.*

*　　　*　　　*

Nicholas Frayling, the Dean, came round first thing the following morning. As a fellow musician he had loved and respected Anne. He has been a tower of strength to me ever since. Eventually the funeral arrangements were made: a Solemn (sung) Requiem in the cathedral, followed by a burial in the family area of Heyshott churchyard. I asked for the Widor Mass and our cathedral choir. I also asked Nicholas to preach and conduct the service and suggested the hymns. Alan Thurlow had a problem on his hands: the cathedral organ was out of commission, but Mark Wardell agreed to play the Mass on the Allen organ, now at the west end of the cathedral, and Alan arranged for his choir also to be situated there in front of the west door. The whole service would therefore be in the nave.

Anne was brought into the cathedral the previous evening when Tim took the brief service. She rested in the chapel of St Mary Magdalene overnight.

The weather was good the next morning and the sun continued to shine all day. Many friends began arriving and I asked the family to assemble in the house. Obviously I had been shattered by Anne's death, but the love and prayers of the cathedral community, joined with those of family and friends, upheld me and turned my sorrowful mourning into a joyful thanksgiving for all the love and life and faith Anne and I had shared over all the years. I knew there would still be times of weeping – and there were – and in some ways, one never gets over it. But life goes on and steadily gets better. It was with these and other thoughts and prayers that I faced and, to be honest, rather dreaded this day.

In fact, from the first moment of entering the cathedral, I felt uplifted, both by the sight of the nave filled with family and friends from far and near, and by the magnificent music and the leading of the service by the priests, with vergers and servers. At the entry of the organ and then of the choir for the Kyrie of the Widor Mass – music I had heard so often with Anne at the keyboard and more lately played by Mark – I was lifted out of this world. The choir, under Alan's wonderful direction, truly sang from the heart.

Nicholas Frayling gave a brilliant address, with a light touch and with humour, but containing a message for us all. The opening words set the tone:

The 15th evening will never be the same again in Chichester: Anne, sitting with her head down, mouthing all 73 verses of Psalm 78 – from memory of course – and looking up, her face alight with joy at a favourite verse or a particularly immoderate use of the organ. Her particular favourites were the hot thunderbolts in verse 49, and the closing verses of the psalm, where young David was taken by God from the sheep-folds, and led his people with a faithful and true heart. Anne's fingers and feet were seldom idle as she instinctively played the accompaniment to some setting, or a Bach fugue or the great Toccata of her beloved Widor; for Anne was a consummate artist, and a musician – literally – to her fingertips . . . Anne possessed a formidable technique and as Hawkins, a pupil of Widor, said of his pupil and assistant, she was able to play the master's music 'with the master's interpretation'.

The Dean then outlined Anne's career both before and after her marriage. He closed by saying that she was

> . . . waiting for that perfecting and peace which lie beyond human weakness and frailty, where the jagged bits and the discords of this life give way to one equal light and one equal music in the fullness of eternity.
>
> That is our prayer for Anne today – just as she would wish – and it is coupled with one equal prayer for Morris, whose life has been so bound up with Anne's for so long, and to such wonderful effect.

His words in the context of such a glorious Eucharist were an inspiration to me as I walked out behind Anne's earthly remains, with our cousins Sue and Helen on each side and both families close behind. Her beloved musicians lined the route in the cloisters and we walked down St Richard's Walk, our first walk together as husband and wife just 51 years before. We then all drove away to Heyshott, Jeremy having made a quick change out of his cassock and surplice, and marshalling my family and their cars.

The committal, a simple service, beautiful in its brevity, was conducted by dear John Manchester, now a Canon of York. We all sprinkled earth on the coffin. After a lingering look, we then adjourned to Sue's house for a quiet reception with all the family. They were all a very great support to me.

After a fulfilling and fulfilled life on earth, my darling Anne is at rest in Christ. May he raise her up, with us all, on the last day.

Epilogue

The *Daily Telegraph* and *The Times* both carried sizeable obituaries, each with a photograph of Anne at the keyboard. The former described her as 'a prominent cathedral organist and an outstanding bishop's wife'. She deserved both accolades. The latter also outlined her career as an 'accomplished organist . . . the first woman in that role in a British cathedral'. It also told of her later becoming 'a much loved figure in parish life . . . thanks to a mixture of determination, humility and joyful laughter . . . Among her enthusiasms were the natural world and lunching in good hostelries.'

The letters poured in, and in the end I replied by hand to over 400. Some were very moving and spoke of Anne as 'such a wonderful lady – she will be greatly missed' (a cathedral verger) and of her 'always being so kind and gentle' (a York vice-principal) and 'such a bubbly and happy person' (a god-daughter). A Canterbury friend wrote, 'I loved your description of her as an encourager: she certainly was that.' Another York friend remembered 'going into the kitchen at Poppleton and being received by a smiling Anne amidst a marvellous smell of apples cooking'.

Others gave emphasis to the partnership. 'We have such happy memories of Anne in our York days and give thanks for your unique and loving partnership which was an

167

example to us all' (ex-diocesan bishop); and 'You were so much together in love and faith. You were such a wonderful partnership and have achieved so much together' (our best man, a retired priest); and again, 'You had a marvellous long life together and have had a magnificent working partnership as well' (ex-Cambridge friend). Another reminisced: 'Anne was a wonderful person in so many ways. I see her now flying along St Richard's Walk in her grey cloak, full of energy and vitality and so attractive' (old Chichester friend) and finally, 'She came out to Cayton to give a recital after our little chamber organ was restored. I also remember with affection the hospitality of St Martin's Vicarage we enjoyed there . . . What a helpmeet Anne has been to you and how marvellous to have done so much of your ministry together – a cause of wonderful thanksgiving to so very many people' (a priest friend from Scarborough days). All this made me realize more than ever that our marriage was made in heaven, for God had a work for us to do and gave us grace to do it *together*. In fact neither of us could have accomplished it alone: we could only have done it by God's grace in this 'unique and loving partnership'.

Once the letters were answered, I suppose the adrenalin ceased to flow and I collapsed at a petrol station. I was taken to hospital and found to have a deficient heart valve. I was very impressed with the standards of the NHS, the first time I had been on the receiving end in a hospital. Sue and Steve, Helen, Jeremy, Clare Feaver and both Tim Schofield and the chaplain paid visits. Gareth Tuckwell generously arranged a week in the Burrswood hospital wing as convalescence and Helen drove me there and came and fetched me. Again, the care of the doctors, nurses and chaplains was of a very high standard.

Once home, the love of the cathedral community, relations and friends sustained me and I began to take courage and grow in strength. Sue and Clare shopped for me each week. The only extra prescription was a daily aspirin and my cardiologist arranged to see me after three months and then after six. I walked every day. The pain of the bereavement began to ease, but I missed Anne terribly at every turn and, although it may get better, the loss will never go away. Thank God for one's faith and the regular receiving of Christ's sacrament and the daily offices! As always, it was wonderful to have the cathedral, its priests and people, close at hand.

Gradually I regained strength and became fitter and had an enjoyable Easter both in Chichester and Heyshott with Anne's family.

The turning point was a trip to Worcester for a few days to see my neighbour, Peter Atkinson, installed as Dean. Again Helen drove me, and it was delightful to find that my bedroom window looked out on to the beautiful Malvern Hills. I was able to robe for the installation service and processed in with my fellow bishops, followed by the Dean and Chapter of Chichester. As always, Peter preached a brilliant sermon. Afterwards at the reception on the cathedral green – where there seemed to be as many Chichester as Worcester people – we enjoyed glorious late-April sunshine. (Those four days were later to be known as the '2007 summer' – the real summer that followed was the wettest in England since 1912!) We returned for the Sunday Eucharist – again an excellent and humorous sermon from Peter, who was welcomed by the Chapter and congregation.

On the previous Friday Helen and I had visited Elgar's birthplace and museum – we are both devotees of Elgar – and on the Sunday afternoon walked on the Malvern Hills, stopping to drink the water at the holy well. We finished up with tea at the Cottage in the Wood above Malvern Wells. The following day we drove home through the Cotswolds,

pausing for coffee appropriately at the Lygon Arms in
Broadway – the Lygon family is associated with the thirteenth variation of the Enigma.

My health had improved, and two more holidays in
August were to increase my sense of well-being. The first was
in Yorkshire with Jeremy, who kindly drove me in my car
round all the old haunts. We began in Kirkburton, my
father's last parish, then travelled on to Elland (via Dobson's
sweet shop/factory to collect the church key), and there visited my father's grave. All the time, I noticed that Jeremy was
taking photographs.

After pausing for a day in York to see my beloved Minster,
we arrived at Old Malton, where John Manchester gave us a
warm welcome. A feature of our visit to John was saying the
daily offices with him in his priory church. In between trips
to well-appointed hostelries (he must have caught the habit
from us!), he took us to several places, including Selby
Abbey. It was a joy to find the Abbey so well kept, and good
to see the family window in the north quire aisle where it had
been placed on St Paul's Day, 1978. Other visits were to St
Martin-on-the-Hill, Scarborough – Jeremy and I took Mary,
my only surviving cousin on my father's side, out to lunch at
the Crown – and to Weaverthorpe and Helperthorpe where
we lunched with Anne's god-daughter, Helen Milner, and
her husband Anthony, at their farm between the two
churches. On the Saturday, Leslie Stanbridge gathered our
healing prayer fellowship, now in its 33rd year, in John's
Priory Church, and it was a great privilege to celebrate the
Eucharist and speak to them once again. In the evening, we
went to see Mick and Lucy Willoughby, three of whose
children I had baptized: two of them introduced us to their
spouses and 22 of us sat down to dinner! Sunday saw us at
the Minster for Evensong when John robed and sat in his
stall and I sat in my old 'Selby'one.

After this we went on to stay a couple of nights at Settrington with Richard and Virginia Storey, always generous hosts. Among their guests for dinner were James Jones, Bishop of Liverpool, and Nigel Forbes Adam, an old Cambridge friend. I had an enjoyable chat with both of them. At the end of the holiday, Jeremy very unexpectedly presented me with a fine album of all the photographs he had taken and secretly had printed. I had wondered why he so often went 'shopping'! So ended my second enjoyable holiday of the year. There was one yet to come.

Before that, I had two main projects to accomplish at home. The first was the signing of the contract for this book and a trip to SPCK in Causton Street, London, to see my editor, Alison Barr. It was an exciting moment. The other was to make arrangements with the cathedral authorities to move to the flat upstairs, where our old bedrooms had been made into excellent accommodation. In this I was to receive great assistance from Wendy in the clearing and cleaning up of the old flat, from Helen for ideas and new furnishings, and from Jeremy who, with them, eventually helped me to move. David Mowlam, the cathedral communar, his assistant Annabelle Winship, and Simon, one of the cathedral gardeners, were also most obliging.

The third holiday was in Helen's lovely house on Hayling Island which looks across the sea to Chichester Cathedral and its Sussex Downs backdrop. In fact, from the balcony, where we had many sunny breakfasts, one can see the whole range of the Downs from Butser to Bignor. I also went there for another purpose, to continue writing this book, which I completed by the end of the holiday.

Returning home to Chichester and its cathedral community, there was Christian joy in my heart as I prepared for the beginning of a new chapter.

Postscript

St Richard's Hospital
Chichester PO19
14/12/07

Dear Alison

Very many thanks for your Christmas card and greetings.

As you see, I am in hospital. Rather inconveniently, I collapsed in the Cathedral 2 mins before Evensong on Advent Sunday (good place to do it though!). The result of the tests here is that I face a triple by-pass and valve replacement (I knew about the valve) in Southampton General on Christmas Eve! Meanwhile I am confined to barracks here. I feel perfectly well and face the prospect with equanimity. I have got Jeremy to bring in the MS in the *hope* I can do some work meanwhile. Helen and he are wonderful and I am well cared for and prayed for.

But I'm afraid this means a postponement of dates because I want to continue in earnest when I am fit. I'm sure you will understand. So sorry about this hiatus. Jeremy or I will be in touch.

May I wish you some rest and *perhaps* a holiday? And may you have a truly blessed Christmas & Hogmanay. Thank you *so much* for your card.

As ever

Morris

★ ★ ★

173

Morris seemed to be recovering well from heart surgery when he returned to Chichester early in the new year. Sadly, he suffered a relapse and died on 19 January 2008.